Instructor's Manual and Test Bank to Accompany

FIFTH EDITION

TEN STEPS
to
ADVANCING
COLLEGE
READING SKILLS

John Langan

ATLANTIC CAPE COMMUNITY COLLEGE

TP

Books in the Townsend Press Reading Series:

Groundwork for College Reading with Phonics
Groundwork for College Reading
Ten Steps to Building College Reading Skills
Ten Steps to Improving College Reading Skills
Ten Steps to Advancing College Reading Skills
Ten Steps to Advanced Reading

Books in the Townsend Press Vocabulary Series:

Vocabulary Basics
Groundwork for a Better Vocabulary
Building Vocabulary Skills
Building Vocabulary Skills, Short Version
Improving Vocabulary Skills
Improving Vocabulary Skills, Short Version
Advancing Vocabulary Skills
Advancing Vocabulary Skills, Short Version
Advanced Word Power

Supplements Available for Most Books:

Instructor's Edition
Instructor's Manual and Test Bank
Online Exercises
PowerPoint Slides

Copyright © 2010 by Townsend Press, Inc.
Printed in the United States of America
9 8 7 6 5 4 3 2 1

ISBN-13: 978-1-59194-214-6
ISBN-10: 1-59194-214-4

For book orders and requests for desk copies or supplements, contact us in any of the following ways:

By telephone: 1-800-772-6410

By fax: 1-800-225-8894

By e-mail: cs@townsendpress.com

Through our website: www.townsendpress.com

CONTENTS

MODEL NOTES AND ACTIVITIES FOR "FOUR ADDITIONAL READINGS"   43

TEST BANK   53

Note: There are four mastery tests for each skill, supplementing the six mastery tests in the book itself. These tests can be used at a variety of points along the student's path of working through the chapter and the mastery tests in the book.

NOTES FOR INSTRUCTORS

On the first three pages of the Instructor's Edition of *Ten Steps to Advancing College Reading Skills*, Fifth Edition, I list some hints for teaching a reading course and for using the book. I add here some other comments.

Using a Class Contract

In the first class of the semester, I explain to students that I regard the course as a serious, professional relationship between them and me. I say that I want them to sign a professional contract for taking the course. I then pass out a contract for them to read and sign.

In my experience, the contract helps motivate younger students in particular to come to class and to assume responsibility for their own learning. Some of the older students don't need such a contract, but they welcome a clear presentation of basic ground rules regarding attendance and grading in the course.

A copy of the contract appears on pages 6–7; you have permission to modify and use this contract in whatever way you see fit.

Supplements for the Book

There are five supplements for the book:

- An *Instructor's Edition,* which is identical to the student book except that it provides the answers to all of the practices and tests.
- The combined *Instructor's Manual and Test Bank,* which you are now reading.
- *Online exercises* consisting of two additional mastery tests for each skill plus two combined-skills tests—22 tests in all. These online tests are free for students and instructors using the book and may be accessed at the Online Learning Center area of **www.townsendpress.com**.
- *PowerPoint slides* and *Blackboard cartridges,* available in the "Supplements" area for instructors at **www.townsendpress.com**.

If you've adopted *Ten Steps to Advancing College Reading Skills* for use in your reading classes, you're entitled to free copies of the two print supplements. Call 1-800-772-6410 or e-mail us at **cs@townsendpress.com** to get them shipped out to you immediately.

A Suggested Syllabus

Weeks 1–10:

One way to begin using the book is to have students read and discuss "How to Become a Better Reader and Thinker" on pages 3–8 and "The Power of Reading" on pages 11–12. Urge your students to take advantage of the book offer on pages 12–13. Then, as the first homework assignment, ask them to read the essay "The Professor Is a Dropout" on pages 459–473. Discuss the questions on page 473 in the next class.

I suggest then teaching one chapter a week, following the order in the book. Generally at the end of a chapter I give two mastery tests: one for practice and one that counts for a grade.

I go over the tests in class right after students take them. (I recommend collecting test papers as students finish and distributing them to students in other parts of the room. Some students resist putting X's on a paper that belongs to the person sitting right next to them.) That way students get immediate feedback on how they have done. Also, after class all I need to do is to check the grades quickly and transfer them to my grade book.

As the semester progresses, I use additional mastery tests, every so often, to review previous skills covered in the class.

Weeks 11–15:

In the last five weeks, students read two selections a week from Part Two of the book. They also do the remaining mastery tests, including some of the tests in this manual, as well as the combined-skills tests in the book and in this manual.

Having done all of the reading of the materials in the book, as well as all of the thinking required to complete the many activities, students are, in my experience, better readers and thinkers. They are better equipped both to handle a standardized reading test at the semester's end and to go on to content courses in their college curriculum.

Suggested Answers to the Discussion Questions

Pages 23–42 in this manual provide suggested answers to the discussion questions that follow each of the twenty readings in Parts One and Two of the book. There was simply no room in the Instructor's Edition for this material.

Writing Assignments

Writing and reading are closely related skills: practice at one will make a student better at the other. Also, writing about a selection is an excellent way of thinking about it. For these reasons, three writing assignments are provided (beginning on page 675 of the book) for each of the twenty reading selections in Parts One and Two.

If you ask students to write about a selection, I suggest you first have them read the "Brief Guide to Effective Writing" that appears on pages 673–674.

Teaching Vocabulary

One basic change that I've made in my teaching of reading is that I now directly teach vocabulary. We all know that students don't know enough words. Because they don't, they have trouble understanding what they read, and they're limited in what they can write. (We have all seen how, in standardized reading tests, students are frustrated because they don't know enough of the words in a passage to understand it and to answer comprehension questions about it. And we all know that because of the vocabulary problem, the standardized tests that are intended to measure reading comprehension are often in fact serving as vocabulary tests.)

I teach vocabulary using a words-in-context approach (it is of no value to ask students to memorize isolated lists of vocabulary words). Specifically, I use a book titled *Advancing Vocabulary Skills, Short Version*, by Sherrie Nist. There are twenty chapters in this book, with ten words in each chapter. I do the first chapter in class, so that students understand how to use the pronunciation key for the words and understand just how the chapter works. I then assign one or two chapters a week for homework.

In class each week, I walk around and check students' books to see that they have worked through the four pages of material for each chapter. (After this quick check, I then return the focus of the class to reading skills.) Every third week, I give students one of the several tests that follow each unit of five chapters in the book. My vocabulary syllabus looks like this:

Week 2: Vocabulary chapter 1 covered in class
Week 3: Vocabulary chapters 2–3 for homework
Week 4: Vocabulary chapters 4–5 for homework plus a test on Unit One in class
Week 5: Vocabulary chapters 6–7 for homework
Week 6: Vocabulary chapters 8–9 for homework
Week 7: Vocabulary chapter 10 for homework plus a test on Unit Two in class
Week 8: Vocabulary chapters 11–12 for homework
Week 9: Vocabulary chapters 13–14 for homework
Week 10: Vocabulary chapter 15 for homework plus a test on Unit Three in class
Week 11: Vocabulary chapters 16–17 for homework
Week 12: Vocabulary chapters 18–19 for homework
Week 13: Vocabulary chapter 20 for homework plus a test on Unit Four in class

The Importance of Continual Reading and Thinking

Continual reading—coupled with thinking about what one has read—is the very heart of a reading class. *One improves the skills of reading and thinking by guided reading and thinking.* This statement is emphasized with good reason. If a teacher is not careful, he or she may play too participatory a role in the classroom, getting more reading and thinking practice than the student does. The teacher should serve as a manager, using the materials in the text to give students the skills practice they need. *Ten Steps to Advancing College Reading Skills* helps the teacher ensure that students do a great deal of active reading and thinking in the classroom.

The Importance of Constant Feedback

Along with continual reading, writing, and thinking, it is vital that students get frequent feedback. Here are ways they can secure such feedback:

- Small-group interactions
- Class discussions and reviews
- Short one-on-one sessions with the instructor
- Graded quizzes and tests
- The Limited Answer Key in the back of the book
- The online exercises available at **www.townsendpress.com**

In addition, since instructors using *Ten Steps to Advancing College Reading Skills* as a class text are permitted to reproduce any or all parts of this manual, you can selectively hand out copies of answers included here.

All of the exercises in the book are designed to make it easy to give clear and specific feedback. If students are going to learn to read and think more effectively, then they need clear, logical, specific responses to their efforts. This book enables teachers to provide such feedback.

Outlining, Mapping, and Summarizing

To take thoughtful, effective study notes, students need to learn three essential techniques: outlining, mapping, and summarizing. All three techniques often require students to identify the main idea and the major supporting details of a selection. But while educators agree that these three techniques are important for students to learn, they are all too seldom taught.

The book gives students instruction and practice in all three techniques. Passages in the "Supporting Details" and the two "Relationships" chapters, as well as all of the reading selections in Part Two and the four additional readings in Part Four, are followed by an outlining, a mapping, or a summarizing activity. To complete many of these activities, students must look closely at the basic organization of the selection. They must think carefully about what they have read by asking two key questions: "What is the point?" and "What is the support for that point?" As students apply the techniques from one selection to the next and get specific feedback on their efforts, they will develop their ability to think in a clear and logical way.

Readability Levels . . . and Their Limitations

Below are the readability grade levels for the text of the book itself and the twenty reading selections. Because the book has been prepared on a computer, and there are now software programs that determine readability, it has been possible to do a complete readability evaluation for each reading, rather than merely sampling excerpts from the materials.

Please remember, however, that there are limits to the reliability and validity of readability scores. For instance, a readability formula cannot account for such significant factors as student interest, prior knowledge of a subject, the number of examples provided to explain concepts, and the overall clarity and logic of the writing.

Thus, while "Julia Burney: The Power of a Woman's Dream" has a readability level of 7th grade, it is a sophisticated adult piece that may be more challenging to students than, for example, "He Was First," which has a reading level of 9. And while "How Dual-Earner Couples Cope" has a readability level of 13, its extremely clear organization makes it a piece that developmental students can understand. I respect readability levels, but I also take them with a grain of salt, and I have kept other factors in mind while determining the sequence of readings.

Material	Word Count	Reading Level
Text of *Ten Steps*		9
Part One		
1. All Washed Up?	1377	9
2. How Dual-Earner Couples Cope	927	13
3. Baby Love	1082	11
4. Personal Relationships in the Not-So-Good Old Days	816	10
5. Julia Burney: The Power of a Woman's Dream	3196	7
6. The Influence of the Self-Fulfilling Prophecy	1152	12
7. What Shamu Taught Me	1656	10
8. Hard Times, a Helping Hand	1536	10
9. Obedience: Milgram's Controversial Studies	1081	10
10. Managing Conflicts in Relationships	1831	10

A Final Note

Writing a book that contains hundreds of explanations and activities is a bit like being in a ball game where one steps up to the batter's box an almost countless number of times. One tries to get as many hits and extra-base hits as possible: to explain every concept so that students really understand it; to provide readings and practices that both interest students and teach the skills. One tries not to hit any foul balls. Hopefully there are not too many in this Fifth Edition of a book that has benefited from a great deal of teacher and student feedback.

Realistically, though, you might find that despite my best efforts, some items may not work. If they don't, and/or if you or your students are confused or uncertain about certain items, let me know so that I can consider making changes in the next printing or revision of the book. Send a note to me at Townsend Press, 439 Kelley Drive, West Berlin, NJ 08091. Alternatively, call Townsend Press at its toll-free number: 1-800-772-6410; send a fax to 1-800-225-8894; or send e-mail to **cs@townsendpress.com**; your comments will be passed on to me. And if you have a question, a Townsend editor will get back to you with an answer very shortly.

My thanks in advance for your help in my effort to keep improving the book!

John Langan

A PROFESSIONAL CONTRACT

FOR FIFTEEN WEEKS TOGETHER

between

_____

(Student's name here)

and

_____

(Instructor's name here)

Welcome to *(name of course)* _____. Counting today, we will be spending fifteen weeks together. How successful we are will depend on how well we follow a business contract that I would like you to read and sign, and that I will then sign and return to you. Here are the terms of the contract.

MY ROLE IN THE CONTRACT

My role will be to help you practice and master important reading and writing and thinking and learning skills. I will try to present these communication skills clearly and to give you interesting and worthwhile practice materials. I will conduct this as a skills course—not a lecture course where you could borrow a friend's notes afterwards. Typically several skills will be explained briefly in class, and you will then spend most of the class time practicing those skills, making them your own. You will be learning in the best possible way: through doing.

Why learn these skills?

I promise you that the skills will be of real value to you in all the other courses you take in college. They will make you a better reader, writer, thinker, and learner, and they can dramatically increase your chance for success in school.

The skills can be just as valuable for the career work you are likely to do in the future. Consider that America is no longer an industrial society where many people work on farms or in factories. Instead, most jobs now involve providing services or processing information. More than ever, communication skills are the tools of our trade. This course will be concerned directly with helping you learn and strengthen the communication skills that will be vital for job success in the 21st century.

YOUR ROLE IN THE CONTRACT

Experiencing the course

Your role in this contract will be to come to every class and to give a full effort. Much of the value and meaning of this skills course will come from what happens in class, so you must be here on a steady basis. Imagine trying to learn another skill without being present: for example, imagine learning how to drive without the *experience* of actually being in the car and working with the controls and getting feedback from your instructor. How much would you learn about the skill of driving if you relied only on the notes of a classmate? In a similar way, to really learn communication skills, you need direct experience and practice. So if you miss classes, you are in effect missing the course.

Shaping your attitude

Some people start college with a "high-school mindset." They are passive; they do the minimum they need to get by; their attention is elsewhere; they are like the living dead—and the American high-school system (and watching thousands of hours of television) may be to blame. Gradually these people realize that college is not high school: they don't have to be in college, and they are no longer part of the sad game played out in many high schools, where they receive a free ride and promotion no matter how little they do.

If your attitude about learning has been hurt by what happened in high school, then part of your role is to change your attitude. You can do so, and this contract will help.

Understanding sick days and personal days

You should try not to miss *any* classes. But in the professional environment of this class, like in the work world, everyone is entitled to a set number of sick days as well as "personal days"—unexplained absences. In this course, you will have a total of *(insert number)* _____ such days—which can cover such real-world happenings as sickness, car breakdowns, or even the death of someone you know. If you missed more than this amount of time in a real-world job contract, you would be let go. (Only in some extraordinary situation, such as an extended illness confirmed by a doctor's report, might an exception apply.) The professional terms of the work world will apply here: if you miss more than _____ classes, you cannot pass the course.

YOUR ROLE IF YOU MISS CLASS

If you do miss a class, you are responsible for getting the homework for the following week's class. To do so, call a classmate. Write down the names and phone numbers of two people in the room. (For now, use the people sitting on either side of you; you can always change these names later.)

Classmate # 1: *Name* _____   *Phone* _____

Classmate # 2: *Name* _____   *Phone* _____

Note that you **must** turn in all homework assignments or you **cannot pass the course**.

If a test or tests are given on a day you miss class, you cannot ordinarily make up these tests. Instead, you will receive a grade of M (Missing) for each missed test. When all your grades are averaged at the end of the semester, three M's will be omitted; the rest will convert to zeros.

YOUR COMMITMENT

I've read this contract, and the terms seem fair to me. (I like the fact that this college class is being treated as a professional situation, and I'm learning the ground rules up front.) I accept the responsibility and the challenge to make this course worth my time and money.

_____   _____

Signed by (your name here)   *Date*

_____

Witnessed by the instructor

OR: If you don't want to sign this, please meet with me after this class to talk about why.

ANSWERS TO THE TESTS IN THE BOOK

Answers to the Review and Mastery Tests in Part One

VOCABULARY IN CONTEXT:
Review Test 1
1. context clues   4. C
2. B   5. examples
3. A

VOCABULARY IN CONTEXT:
Review Test 4
1. B   6. B
2. A   7. B
3. D   8. A
4. D   9. D
5. C   10. D

VOCABULARY IN CONTEXT:
Review Test 2
A. 1. C   C. 6. D lack of essentials
    2. B   7. E sociable
B. 3. D   8. C insulting
    4. B   9. B continuous
    5. A   10. A by chance

VOCABULARY IN CONTEXT:
Review Test 3
(Wording of answers may vary.)
A. 1. innocent
    2. repeat
    3. guess
    4. relevant *or* applicable
    5. strong
B. 6. negatively *or* unfavorably
    7. weakening
    8. despair
    9. false name *or* pen name
    10. judgments

VOCABULARY IN CONTEXT:
Mastery Test 1
A. 1. A   D. 7. C
B. 2. B   8. B
    3. A   E. 9. A
    4. A   10. C
C. 5. support
    6. prevent

VOCABULARY IN CONTEXT:
Mastery Test 2
A. 1. B   D. 6. A
B. 2. B   7. B
    3. D   8. B
C. 4. change E. 9. D
    5. avoided 10. B

VOCABULARY IN CONTEXT:
Mastery Test 3
A. 1. C   6. C
B. 2. C   7. B
    3. B   8. D
    4. C   9. C
    5. D   10. D

VOCABULARY IN CONTEXT:
Mastery Test 4
1. C   6. A
2. A   7. B
3. A   8. B
4. D   9. A
5. B   10. C

VOCABULARY IN CONTEXT:
Mastery Test 5
A. 1. D
    2. C
    3. D
    4. B
    5. A
B. *(Wording of answers may vary.)*
    6. main
    7. tell apart
    8. keeps in
    9. looking back
    10. somewhat changed

VOCABULARY IN CONTEXT:
Mastery Test 6
A. 1. E death
    2. J said to be caused by
    3. A adjust
    4. G disaster
    5. I put forth as a theory
B. 6. A excited
    7. I strict
    8. G something very popular
    9. C had a strong desire
    10. J unequaled

MAIN IDEAS:
Review Test 1

1. point   4. list words
2. topic   5. beginning
3. C

MAIN IDEAS:
Review Test 4

1. B   6. A
2. C   7. A
3. A   8. B
4. D   9. C
5. A   10. A

MAIN IDEAS:
Review Test 2

A. 1. A. S   B. *Group 1*
      B. P   A. SD
      C. S   B. T
      D. S   C. SD
   2. A. S   D. MI
      B. S   *Group 2*
      C. S   A. SD
      D. P   B. MI
                     C. T
                     D. SD

MAIN IDEAS:
Review Test 3

A. 1. 1
   2. 2
   3. 5
B. 4. 8

MAIN IDEAS:
Mastery Test 1

A. 1. A. P   B. *Group 1*
      B. S   A. MI
      C. S   B. T
      D. S   C. SD
   2. A. S   D. SD
      B. S   *Group 2*
      C. S   A. SD
      D. P   B. T
   3. A. S   C. SD
      B. P   D. MI
      C. S
      D. S

MAIN IDEAS:
Mastery Test 2

A. 1. A. S   B. *Group 1*
      B. P   A. MI
      C. S   B. T
      D. S   C. SD
   2. A. S   D. SD
      B. S   *Group 2*
      C. S   A. SD
      D. P   B. T
   3. A. P   C. MI
      B. S   D. SD
      C. S
      D. S

MAIN IDEAS:
Mastery Test 3

1. 1
2. 2
3. 5
4. 2
5. 3

MAIN IDEAS:
Mastery Test 4

1. 2
2. 7
3. 4
4. 1
5. 3

MAIN IDEAS:
Mastery Test 5

1. 1
2. 2
3. 8
4. 2

MAIN IDEAS:
Mastery Test 6

1. 7
2. 1
3. 11
4. 3

SUPPORTING DETAILS:
Review Test 1
1. details   4. map
2. details   5. examples
3. main ideas

SUPPORTING DETAILS:
Review Test 4
1. D
2. B
3. B
4. B
5. A
6. B
7. A
8–10. A. 1. C
       B.   A
       B. 2. B

SUPPORTING DETAILS:
Review Test 2
A. 1. A   4. A
   2. Also   5. B
   3. In addition

B. *Main idea:* Biological factors affect how warm or cold you feel.
   Major detail: 1. Weight
   Major detail: 2. Muscle mass
      Minor detail: More muscle mass, better you regulate body temperature.
   Major detail: 5. Stress
C. 10. B

(In all these tests, wording of main ideas and supporting details may vary.)

SUPPORTING DETAILS:
Review Test 3
A. . . . functional illiteracy.

Educational   Community   Home
system

B. *Main idea:* There are three mechanisms of heat transfer.
   Major detail: Conduction—heat transferred through matter by molecular activity
   Major detail: Convection—transfer of heat by mass movement within a substance
      Minor detail: water boiling in pan
   Major detail: Radiation—heat that travels out in all directions from its source
C. 10. B

SUPPORTING DETAILS:
Mastery Test 1
A. 1. A   3. B
   2. C   4. B
B. *Main idea:* Herbert Gans identified five basic types of urban dwellers.
   1. Cosmopolites
   2. Singles
   3. Ethnic villagers
   4. Deprived
   5. Trapped

(In all these tests, wording of main ideas and supporting details may vary.)

SUPPORTING DETAILS:
Mastery Test 2
A. 1. D   4. B
   2. C   5. C
   3. A   6. quality
B. 1. Interview
      a. Can obtain a high response rate because people find it difficult to turn down a personal request
   2. Questionnaires
      a. Cheaper than interviews, especially when large samples are used

SUPPORTING DETAILS:
Mastery Test 3
A. 1. B   4. D
   2. D   5. C
   3. C
B.   Duration
      Predictability
      Frame of mind
      Environmental setting
      Attitude

SUPPORTING DETAILS:
Mastery Test 4
A. *Main idea:* People progress through a sequence of stages as they make changes in their lives.
   1. Precontemplation
   2. Contemplation
   3. Preparation
   4. Action
   5. Maintenance
B. *Main idea:* Today's homelessness has arisen from at least three social forces.

Increased   Decreasing   Decrease in
shortage of   demand for   public
inexpensive   unskilled   welfare
housing   labor   benefits
for the poor

SUPPORTING DETAILS:
Mastery Test 5
A. 1. A   3. B
   2. C   4. C
   5. *Ex.*—On a multiple-choice test, eliminate the obviously incorrect answers to each question.
   6. *Ex.*—Break down the writing of a paper into a series of separate tasks: choosing a topic, doing the research, preparing an outline, etc.
B. *Main idea:* Public speaking is very different from everyday conversation.

More   More   Different
structured   formal   method of
               language   delivery

SUPPORTING DETAILS:
Mastery Test 6
A. *Main idea:* There are three forms of plagiarism.
— Global—stealing words and ideas
— Patchwork—stealing from several sources
— Incremental—stealing small portions from different parts of one source
B. *Main idea:* Most forgetting occurs because of interference from other information, which can take place in two ways.
   1. Proactive interference—prior information blocks new information
   2. Retroactive interference—new information blocks old information
C. *Main idea:* There are stages to children's play.
   1. Solitary play—individual play runs an independent course
   2. Parallel play—children play with similar materials near one another, but hardly interact
   3. Cooperative play—direct interaction and cooperative role-taking

IMPLIED MAIN IDEAS:
Review Test 1

1. imply   4. point (*or* idea)
2. topic   5. implied
3. support

IMPLIED MAIN IDEAS:
Review Test 4

1. C   9. D
2. B   10. A
3. B
4. C
5. A
6. D
7. C
8. The primary unit of society and attachment was the peer group.

IMPLIED MAIN IDEAS:
Review Test 2

A. 1. A
B. 2. B
    3. C
    4. We all need to feel we are of use.

(*In all these tests, wording of implied main ideas may vary.*)

IMPLIED MAIN IDEAS:
Review Test 3

A. 1. C
    2. A
B. 3. The hippo is a dangerous animal.
C. 4. D

IMPLIED MAIN IDEAS:
Mastery Test 1

1. C
2. A
3. B
4. A

IMPLIED MAIN IDEAS:
Mastery Test 2

1. A
2. D
3. A
4. D

IMPLIED MAIN IDEAS:
Mastery Test 3

A. 1. D
    2. B
    3. C
B. Americans worry about the wrong things.
    (*Wording of answer may vary.*)

IMPLIED MAIN IDEAS:
Mastery Test 4

A. 1. C
    2. D
B. 3. In our daily lives, we use three kinds of memory.
    4. For an older person living alone, there are many advantages to having a dog.
    (*Wording of answers may vary.*)

IMPLIED MAIN IDEAS:
Mastery Test 5

A. 1. B
    2. A
    3. A
B. 4. A

IMPLIED MAIN IDEAS:
Mastery Test 6

A. C
B. A

RELATIONSHIPS I:
Review Test 1
1. Transitions
2. addition
3. time
4. supporting details
5. pattern of organization

RELATIONSHIPS I:
Review Test 4
1. A   6. B
2. C   7. A
3. B   8. B
4. A   9. B
5. D   10. A

RELATIONSHIPS I:
Review Test 2
A. 1. A   C. 6. B
   2. B   7. After
B. 3. B also   8. Then
   4. C Before   9. Finally
   5. A After   10. B

RELATIONSHIPS I:
Review Test 3
A. 1. First   B. 6. B
   2. Next   7. A
   3. until   8. B
   4. while   9. A
   5. B   10. B

RELATIONSHIPS I:
Mastery Test 1
A. 1. C For one thing
   2. A After   7. second
   3. D later   8. Also
   4. B another   9. final
   5. E soon   10. A
B. 6. First of all

RELATIONSHIPS I:
Mastery Test 2
A. 1. D Before   B. 6. B
   2. E eventually C. 7. finally
   3. C Another   8. then
   4. A After   9. During
   5. B Also   10. B

(In Tests 3–6, wording of main ideas and supporting details may vary.)

RELATIONSHIPS I:
Mastery Test 3
A. 1–4. 2, 3, 1, 4
   5. A
B. 6. B
C. 7. A
   8–10. *Main idea:* Many theories exist about what causes people to commit crimes.
      1. Celebration of violence in our culture
      3. Psychological reasons

RELATIONSHIPS I:
Mastery Test 4
A. 1–4. 4, 1, 3, 2
   5. C
B. 6. C
C. *Main idea:* Several types of marriage occur throughout the world.

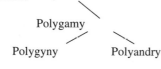

Polygamy
Polygyny   Polyandry

RELATIONSHIPS I:
Mastery Test 5
A. 1. B
   2. *Any of the following:* first, Next, Then, then, Finally
B. 3. A
   4. *Any of the following:* One, Another, also, further
C. 5. A
   6. final
7–10. *Main idea:* There are three main ways of responding to offensive or annoying people.

Passive behavior   Aggressive behavior   Assertive behavior

RELATIONSHIPS I:
Mastery Test 6
A. 1. A
   2. another
   3. B
B. 4. B
   5–7. *Any three of the following:* First, Then, Next, Eventually, Finally
C. 8. A
   9–10. 2. Strengthens the ties between insiders
      4. Gives members a sense of belonging and raises their self-esteem

13

RELATIONSHIPS II:
Review Test 1

1. A   4. C
2. B   5. examples
3. B

RELATIONSHIPS II:
Review Test 4

1. D   6. D
2. B   7. A
3. A   8. B
4. A   9. A
5. C   10. D

RELATIONSHIPS II:
Mastery Test 1

A. 1. D similar   B. 6. A
    2. B For example   7. D
    3. C. In contrast   8. C
    4. E. Therefore   9. B
    5. A. because   10. C

RELATIONSHIPS II:
Mastery Test 4

A. 1–4. 3, 4, 2, 1
     5. C
B.   6. B
     7. B
     8. in common / Both / both / just as /
        Similarly
C.   9. B
    10. effects / caused / Because of /
        due to / as a result

*(In Tests 5 and 6, wording of main ideas
and supporting details may vary.)*

RELATIONSHIPS I and II:
Mastery Test 1

A. 1. C For instance 8. E result
    2. B Finally   9. B for instance
    3. D Later   10. C lastly
    4. E unlike
    5. A because
B. 6. A After
    7. D On the other hand

RELATIONSHIPS II:
Review Test 2

A. 1. D. For instance   B. 6. B
    2. B. Despite   7. C
    3. A. because   8. A
    4. C. even though   9. B
    5. E. Similarly   10. C

RELATIONSHIPS II:
Mastery Test 2

A. 1. D
    2. Differences / On the other hand /
       Unlike / Instead of
B. 3. A
    4. Examples
C. 5. B
    6. effects / Therefore / cause
D. 7. C
    8. similarities / same / like / just as / as
E. 9. B
    10. reasons / led to / explanation /
        resulted in

RELATIONSHIPS II:
Mastery Test 5

A. 1. B
    2–5. Workers are less anxious and
         feel they are part of a community.
         Quality remains high because
         experienced workers are retained.
         Company is better equipped to
         meet increased demand when
         business recovers.
         Workers are more willing to
         put in long hours.
B. 6. C
    7–10. High-*achiever parents*
          Demand independence and
          self-reliance from their children
          at an early age.
          Low-*achiever parents*
          Children are thus less indepen-
          dent and often have low
          achievement needs.

RELATIONSHIPS I and II:
Mastery Test 2

A. 1. C   2. examples / include
B. 3. A   4. For one thing / furthermore
C. 5. B   6. First / Next / Then
D. 7. C   8. consequently / If . . . then /
               therefore / because
E. 9. C   10. similar / differ / however /
               In contrast / Unlike / but /
               Although / difference

RELATIONSHIPS II:
Review Test 3

A. 1. D
    2. leads to / As a result
B. 3. A
    4. For instance / example /
       specifically
C. 5. B
    6. opposite / similarities / likewise /
       just as / Both / different / common
D. 7. C
    8. affect / effect / so
E. 9. B
    10. in contrast / but / However

RELATIONSHIPS II:
Mastery Test 3

A. 1–4. 4, 3, 1, 2
     5. D
B.   6. C
     7. On the other hand / However
     8. On the other hand / However
C.   9. D
    10. For example / including

RELATIONSHIPS II:
Mastery Test 6

A. 1. C
    2–5. *Main idea:* Several reasons
         account for the increase in
         the divorce rate.
         Greater social acceptance of
         divorce
         Increase in family income
         Greater opportunities for women
         (who are thus less dependent on
         their husbands)
B.   6. B
    7–10.

Indirect development	Direct *development*
	1. Juvenile is a sexually immature miniature version of the adult.
	3. Relatively few off-spring are produced.

RELATIONSHIPS I and II:
Mastery Test 3

A. 1. C
B. 2. A
C. 3. C
D. 4. B
E. 5. C

14

INFERENCES:
Review Test 1
1. stated
2. D
3. inferences
4. metaphors
5. tables

INFERENCES:
Review Test 4

1.	A	6.	B
2.	C	7.	D
3.	D	8.	C
4.	D	9.	B
5.	D	10.	A

INFERENCES:
Review Test 2
A. 1, 4, 5, 8
B. 1, 3, 5, 8
C. 2, 3

INFERENCES:
Review Test 3
A. 1, 4, 5, 8
B. 5. A
6. C
7. A
8. A
9. B
10. C

INFERENCES:
Mastery Test 1
A. 1, 4
B. 1, 3
C. 5. C
6. B
7. B
8. A

INFERENCES:
Mastery Test 2
A. 2, 5
B. 3, 5
C. 1, 3, 6, 7, 8, 9

INFERENCES:
Mastery Test 3
A. 2, 5
B. 2, 4, 6, 7
C. 7. A
8. C
9. B
10. C

INFERENCES:
Mastery Test 4
A. 1. C
2. A
3. A
4. B
5. A
B. 1, 3, 4, 7, 10

INFERENCES:
Mastery Test 5
A. 1. C
2. B
3. B
4. D
5. C
B. 1, 4, 6, 7, 9

INFERENCES:
Mastery Test 6
A. 1, 3, 4, 7, 8
B. 2, 4, 6, 9, 10

PURPOSE AND TONE:
Review Test 1

1. A
2. C
3. tones
4. ironic (*or* sarcastic)
5. T

PURPOSE AND TONE:
Review Test 2

1. P   4. P
2. I   5. I
3. E

PURPOSE AND TONE:
Review Test 3

1. F
2. E
3. C
4. H
5. B

PURPOSE AND TONE:
Review Test 4

1. B   6. B
2. D   7. A
3. C   8. B
4. D   9. D
5. A   10. B

PURPOSE AND TONE:
Mastery Test 1

A. 1. I   B. 6. B
    2. P   7. A
    3. E   8. D
    4. I   9. E
    5. E   10. C

PURPOSE AND TONE:
Mastery Test 2

A. 1. P   6. I
    2. E   7. P
    3. I B. 8. C
    4. E   9. A
    5. P   10. D

PURPOSE AND TONE:
Mastery Test 3

A. 1. G   6. E
    2. I   7. H
    3. C   8. B
    4. J B. 9. P
    5. F   10. E

PURPOSE AND TONE:
Mastery Test 4

A. 1. A   6. E
    2. D   7. H
    3. F   8. G
    4. C B. 9. A
    5. B   10. B

PURPOSE AND TONE:
Mastery Test 5

A. 1. B C. 5. B
    2. C   6. D
B 3. B D. 7. B
    4. B   8. A

PURPOSE AND TONE:
Mastery Test 6

A. 1. C C. 5. B
    2. C   6. C
B. 3. B D. 7. A
    4. D   8. D

ARGUMENT:
Review Test 1

1. support *or* evidence
2. Γ
3. relevant
4. adequate
5. What is the support?

ARGUMENT:
Review Test 4

1. B		6. A	
2. C		7. C	
3. B		8. B	
4. C		9. D	
5. D		10. A. S	
		B. X	
		C. P	
		D. S	

ARGUMENT:
Review Test 2

(Wording of answers to items 1 and 2 may vary.)

A. 1. He doesn't want to eat fruits or vegetables because awful things happen to people who do.

    2. An apple poisoned Snow White; the beanstalk led to a threatening giant; the mushroom did bad things to Alice (it made her shrink or grow).

    3. B   C. 8–10. A, C, F

B. 4. B
    5. C
    6. D
    7. A

ARGUMENT:
Review Test 3

A. 1. A
    2. D
    3. C

B. *Group 1*
    4. D
    Group 2
    5. C

ARGUMENT:
Mastery Test 1

A. 1. F   C. 5–7. B, D, E
B. 2. D   8–10. A, C, F
    3. C
    4. C

ARGUMENT:
Mastery Test 2

A. 1. D   B. 5–7. C, D, F
    2. D   8–10. C, E, F
    3. B
    4. B

ARGUMENT:
Mastery Test 3

A. 1–3. B, C, E
    4–6. A, B, E
B. *Group 1*
    7. C
    Group 2
    8. C

ARGUMENT:
Mastery Test 4

A. 1–3. A, B, D
    4–6. B, D, F
B.   7. A
    8. 1
    9. B
    10. A

ARGUMENT:
Mastery Test 5

A. 1. C
B. 2. A
    3. C
    4. A
    5. D

ARGUMENT:
Mastery Test 6

A. 1–3. B, C, E
    4–6. A, B, D
B.   7. B
    8. B
    9. C
    10. D

CRITICAL READING:
Review Test 1
1. T
2. C
3. opinions
4. A
5. F   8. B
6. A   9. T
7. B   10. A

CRITICAL READING:
Review Test 2
1. A   6. F
2. F   7. O
3. O   8. F
4. O   9. F+O
5. F+O   10. F

CRITICAL READING:
Review Test 3
A. 1. A   B. 6. B
2. D   7. A
3. B   8. C
4. D   9. A
5. C   10. C

CRITICAL READING:
Review Test 4
1. A   6. C
2. B   7. C
3. A   8. B
4. B   9. C
5. B   10. A

CRITICAL READING:
Mastery Test 1
A. 1. B   C. 11. O
B. 2. F   12. F+O
3. O   13. F
4. O   14. O
5. F   15. O
6. F   16. F
7. O   17. F
8. F   18. F+O
9. O   19. O
10. F+O   20. F

CRITICAL READING:
Mastery Test 2
A. 1. F   B. 11. F+O
2. F   12. F
3. F   13. O
4. O   14. F
5. F   15. F
6. F+O   16. F+O
7. O   17. F
8. O   18. O
9. F+O   19. F
10. F   20. O

CRITICAL READING:
Mastery Test 3
A. 1. D   B. 7. C
2. B   8. A
3. C   9. F
4. A   10. B
5. D
6. C

CRITICAL READING:
Mastery Test 4
A. 1. B   B. 7. C
2. D   8. F
3. B   9. A
4. C   10. B
5. A
6. D

CRITICAL READING:
Mastery Test 5
A. 1. C   B. 6. C
2. A   7. A
3. B   8. B
4. A   9. A
5. C   10. C

CRITICAL READING:
Mastery Test 6
A. 1. C   B. 6. B
2. B   7. C
3. C   8. B
4. B   9. A
5. A   10. C

Answers to the Reading Selections in Part Two

1 THE PROFESSOR IS A DROPOUT

Skills Questions

1. A	6. A	11. B	16. A
2. C	7. C	12. A	17. C
3. B	8. B	13. D	18. C
4. C	9. D	14. C	19. A
5. B	10. C	15. B	20. D

Summarizing *(Note: Wording of answers may vary.)*
— her grandfather became blind, and the family moved to Brownsville, Texas, hoping that doctors there could help him regain his eyesight
— a teacher and the principal shouted at her because she spoke in Spanish to a man asking for directions
— speaking English at home
— the success of her own children

2 TAMING THE ANGER MONSTER

Skills Questions

1. B	6. C	11. D	16. B
2. A	7. A	12. C	17. B
3. B	8. D	13. A	18. C
4. A	9. B	14. D	19. D
5. C	10. A	15. A	20. A

Outlining *(Note: Wording of answers may vary.)*
B. 1. Time
   2. Technology
   3. Tension
C. 1. Common sense and patience

3 HE WAS FIRST

Skills Questions

1. B	6. F	11. A	16. B
2. C	7. C	12. A	17. Paragraph 3
3. C	8. B	13. T	18. A. S
4. D	9. C	14. C	B. P
5. A	10. C	15. A	C. X
			D. S
			19. A
			20. C

Summarizing *(Note: Wording of answers may vary.)*
— not to fight back if anyone insulted him or attacked him with racial slurs
— accepted him and were friendly to both Jackie and his wife, Rachel
— Jackie had to stay in a "colored" hotel
— other team owners followed Branch Rickey's lead and hired black players, thereby changing major-league baseball forever

4 MY FATHER'S HANDS

Skills Questions

1. B	6. B	11. A	16. C
2. D	7. C	12. D	17. C
3. D	8. D	13. B	18. C
4. B	9. A	14. A	19. C
5. C	10. A	15. B	20. B

Summarizing *(Note: Wording of answers may vary.)*
— he grew restless and gave up
— he could not pass the written qualification test
— if God would refuse him entry into heaven because his hands couldn't write
— his father had been unable to open the bottle because he had been unable to read the directions

5 MOTIVATION AND NEEDS

Skills Questions

1. C	6. B	12. D	17. C
2. A	7. T	13. C	18. A. S
3. C	8. C	14. D	B. X
4. D	9. D	15. T	C. S
5. A	10. C	16. A	D. P
	11. peak experience . . .		19. B
	five		20. F

Mapping

Self-actualization needs
Esteem and self-esteem needs
Love and belongingness needs
Safety and security needs
Stimulation needs

6 EFFECTS OF THE AUTOMOBILE

Skills Questions

1. B	6. B	11. C	16. D
2. C	7. D	12. B	17. A. P
3. A	8. D	13. B	B. S
4. A	9. C	14. C	C. S
5. A	10. D	15. A	18. C
			19. A
			20. D

Summarizing *(Note: Wording of answers may vary.)*
— horses and streetcar lines
— lower taxes
— parents
— women
— technology

7   RABIES

Skills Questions

1. B	6. A	11. B	16. A
2. B	7. C	12. A	17. D
3. symptoms	8. C	13. C	18. C
4. B	9. D	14. T	19. A
5. D	10. D	15. B	20. C

Outlining

A. 2. A booster dose every two years, since antibody
      levels fall with time
B. Prevention for people already bitten by an animal that
    may have rabies
    1. For people not previously immunized
    2. b. Vaccine injections on days 0 and 2

8   BAD MANAGERS

Skills Questions

1. A	6. B	11. A	16. D
2. A	7. B	12. A	17. C
3. B	8. D	13. C	18. T
4. B	9. A	14. B	19. D
5. C	10. D	15. T	20. C

Mapping

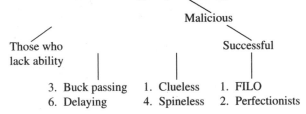

There are two types of bad managers.

Malicious

Those who
lack ability   Successful

3. Buck passing   1. Clueless   1. FILO
6. Delaying   4. Spineless   2. Perfectionists

9   BUSY AS A BEE?

Skills Questions

1. D	6. D	11. C	16. A
2. B	7. C	12. B	17. C
3. A	8. D	13. D	18. A. X
4. C	9. F	14. C	B. S
5. B	10. D	15. D	C. P
			D. S
			19. A
			20. B

Outlining

B

10   STEPPING INTO THE LIGHT

Skills Questions

1. D	6. B	11. B	16. T
2. A	7. D	12. D	17. D
3. C	8. B	13. D	18. C
4. D	9. C	14. B	19. A
5. A	10. D	15. D	20. D

Summarizing *(Note: Wording of answers may vary.)*
— whether he had been afraid of the kind of white people
   who hate blacks
— she had chosen to be heterosexual
— if her decision was based on who she really was or who
   she wanted people to think she was
— that religion should be used to promote love, not hatred
— no laws recognized Sarah's relationship with Laura

Answers to the Combined-Skills Tests in Part Three

COMBINED SKILLS:
Test 1

1. D		5. A
2. B		6. D
3. D		7. B
4. D		8. C

COMBINED SKILLS:
Test 2

1. A		5. B
2. C		6. C
3. A		7. D
4. B		8. D

COMBINED SKILLS:
Test 3

1. A		5. C
2. C		6. B
3. C		7. B
4. C		8. A

COMBINED SKILLS:
Test 4

1. B		5. B
2. C		6. F
3. B		7. C
4. D		8. A

COMBINED SKILLS:
Test 5

1. C		5. D
2. D		6. A
3. B		7. C
4. A		8. C

COMBINED SKILLS:
Test 6

1. C		5. A
2. C		6. D
3. D		7. B
4. A		8. A

COMBINED SKILLS:
Test 7

1. D		5. A
2. B		6. A
3. B		7. C
4. D		8. B

COMBINED SKILLS:
Test 8

1. B		5. B
2. C		6. D
3. D		7. A
4. A		8. D

COMBINED SKILLS:
Test 9

1. D		5. A
2. B		6. B
3. C		7. D
4. C		8. A

COMBINED SKILLS:
Test 10

1. A		5. A
2. B		6. B
3. B		7. A
4. D		8. C

COMBINED SKILLS:
Test 11

1. D		5. C
2. C		6. B
3. D		7. D
4. C		8. A

COMBINED SKILLS:
Test 12

1. D		5. D
2. C		6. C
3. D		7. D
4. B		8. C

COMBINED SKILLS:
Test 13

1. D		5. A
2. A		6. C
3. C		7. B
4. C		8. C

COMBINED SKILLS:
Test 14

1. D		5. B
2. B		6. B
3. D		7. C
4. B		8. B

COMBINED SKILLS:
Test 15

1. A		5. B
2. B		6. C
3. B		7. C
4. D		8. D

COMBINED SKILLS:
Test 16

1. C	5. D
2. B	6. D
3. D	7. B
4. D	8. B

COMBINED SKILLS:
Test 17

1. D	5. D
2. B	6. A
3. A	7. A
4. A	8. B

COMBINED SKILLS:
Test 18

1. D	5. C
2. C	6. A
3. B	7. B
4. D	8. C

COMBINED SKILLS:
Test 19

1. B	5. B
2. C	6. D
3. C	7. B
4. D	8. A

COMBINED SKILLS:
Test 20

1. D	5. B
2. A	6. B
3. D	7. C
4. B	8. A

Answers to the Tests in Part Four

MORE ABOUT SUMMARIZING
AND OUTLINING:
Review Test 1

1. condense
2. the main idea
3. T
4. F
5. T

MORE ABOUT SUMMARIZING
AND OUTLINING:
Review Test 2

A.	1–2.	*Same:* 3, 5
	3–4.	*Same:* 4, 6
	5–6.	*Same:* 4, 6
B.	7.	D
C.	8.	C

MORE ABOUT SUMMARIZING
AND OUTLINING:
Review Test 3

A.	1–2.	*Same:* 1, 6
	3–4.	*Same:* 1, 5
	5–6.	*Same:* 2, 3
B.	7.	B
C.	8.	B

Additional Tests on
FACT AND OPINION:
Mastery Test 1

A.		B.	
1. F		11. F	
2. O		12. O	
3. O		13. F	
4. O		14. O	
5. F		15. F+O	
6. O		16. F	
7. O		17. F	
8. F		18. O	
9. F		19. F	
10. F+O		20. O	

Additional Tests on
FACT AND OPINION:
Mastery Test 2

A.		B.	
1. F		11. F	
2. O		12. O	
3. O		13. F	
4. F		14. F+O	
5. F		15. O	
6. F		16. F	
7. O		17. F	
8. F		18. O	
9. F		19. O	
10. F+O		20. F	

Additional Tests on
FACT AND OPINION:
Mastery Test 3

A.		B.	
1. F+O		11. O	
2. F		12. F	
3. F		13. F	
4. O		14. F+O	
5. F		15. F	
6. O		16. O	
7. O		17. F	
8. F		18. F+O	
9. F+O		19. F	
10. F		20. O	

Additional Tests on
FACT AND OPINION:
Mastery Test 4

A.		B.	
1. O		11. O	
2. F+O		12. F	
3. F		13. F	
4. O		14. O	
5. F		15. F+O	
6. O		16. F	
7. F		17. F	
8. F+O		18. F+O	
9. O		19. F	
10. F		20. O	

UNDERSTANDING BIAS:
Review Test 1

1. T
2. F
3. B
4. C
5. C

UNDERSTANDING BIAS:
Review Test 2

A.	1. B	C.	5. A
	2. B		6. C
B.	3. B	D.	7. B
	4. C		8. B

UNDERSTANDING BIAS:
Review Test 3

A.	1. B	C.	5. A
	2. A		6. A
B.	3. A	D.	7. C
	4. B		8. C

SUGGESTED ANSWERS TO THE DISCUSSION QUESTIONS IN PART ONE

Note: For some questions, additional related questions have been included to enhance class discussion.

1   ALL WASHED UP?

1. About how many times a day—and for how long—do you usually wash your hands? Do you think your hand-washing habits will change as a result of reading this selection? Why or why not?

Answers will vary. Encourage students to describe their current hand-washing routine. If they plan to change that routine, ask what specific parts of this essay persuaded them to do so. If they do not plan to change their routine, ask if they already follow the recommendations given here.

2. Do you agree with Hansen's conclusion that spending more time every day washing your hands will "almost certainly" save you from contracting preventable illnesses? Or are there other factors to take into consideration? Explain.

Answers will vary. Most people agree that hand-washing is a highly effective way of preventing the spread of contagious disease. Other factors that may affect an individual's likelihood of getting sick include how much time he or she spends in germ-laden environments (such as a doctor's office or day-care center), the relative strength of the individual's own immune system (some people have underlying conditions that make them very susceptible to illness), and whether the person practices a healthy lifestyle (getting enough sleep, eating well, exercising, not smoking, etc.)

3. In the course of the selection, Hansen refutes the belief that hot water kills germs. What are some other health theories you've heard that may or may not be true? How could you find out whether or not they are true?

There are many common beliefs about health that are not necessarily rooted in fact. Here are a few examples: Cold weather makes you sick. Going out with wet hair can make you sick. Chicken soup is good for colds. Eating hot, spicy food can ward off colds and flu. You should feed a cold, but starve a fever.

Asking a health professional is one way to determine if a health theory is true. Another would be to check the belief out on the Internet. However, students need to be guided to recognize the difference between a legitimate, trustworthy Internet site and one that passes on erroneous information.

4. Hansen points out that frequent hand-washing and flossing one's teeth are two things that people know they ought to do, but probably don't. Can you add some more examples to this list? What do you think are the main reasons people don't do what they should when it comes to questions of health?

Exercising, eating a healthful diet, getting enough sleep, and quitting smoking are among the most common "shoulds." In general, people do not follow these recommendations because the alternatives seem more gratifying in the short term. On a minute-to-minute basis, for example, it is more enjoyable to eat a candy bar than it is to go to the gym. When people are rushed and under stress, they find it easier to focus on short-term pleasure than on the longer-term goal of better health.

2 HOW DUAL-EARNER COUPLES COPE

1. *Discuss some of the challenges in a dual-income marriage. Draw upon your own experience if you are married, or use the example of a married couple you know.*

Students might mention some of the following:

- Dual-earner couples have less time and energy to devote to their home life. It may be more of a challenge to make a house feel like a home when they are both away so much.

- Parents who both work will have to arrange alternate care for their children. Children and parents can both lose out on valuable time spent together.

- The demands of two careers can create conflict. One partner may get an opportunity for advancement that requires a move away from where the other works.

- Partners who both work may become jealous and stressed if one makes more money or is more successful than the other.

- Partners may struggle over how to adapt traditional marriage roles when both partners work. For instance, a husband may continue to regard housework as "women's work" even though his wife is working outside the home.

2. *Discuss some of the benefits in a dual-income marriage. Again, draw upon your own experience if you are married, or use the example of a married couple you know.*

Some points that students may bring up:

- Financial pressure can be hard on a marriage. Having both partners working can relieve that pressure and thereby improve the marriage.

- In a traditional, one-income marriage, each partner may secretly suspect that he or she has the more difficult role. If both work outside the home and share chores at home, each may develop a new appreciation for what the other does.

- Women who have typically stayed home may find their self-esteem growing when they succeed in a job outside the home.

- Men may feel relieved from the stress of having to be a family's sole support.

3. *The author states, "Dual-income couples fall into three patterns: conventional, modern, and role sharing." What view of marriage did your family have as you grew up? How did that view affect your family's lifestyle? If you're married, which view do you and your spouse have?*

Answers will vary. Encourage students to give examples of how they or their families fall into a particular category.

4. *How do you think dual-earner marriages affect children? What, if anything, can spouses who both work outside the home do to ensure that their children receive the time and attention they deserve?*

Some possible effects: Children may benefit if their family is better-off financially. If parents are challenged and satisfied by their work and not so worried about money, their sense of well-being will have a good effect on the home. Children of dual-income marriages grow up knowing that mothers as well as fathers are able to make their own living. If both parents work, children may lose some of the closeness and attention that is available from a stay-at-home parent. They may resent their parents' absence from the home. Parents who work outside the home may not as quickly notice children's problems as they would if they spent more time with the children. Children who are home alone as their parents work may be tempted to get involved in destructive activities.

Answers to the second part of the question will vary.

How can parents take advantage of the good points of a dual-income marriage for their children while minimizing the bad points?

3   BABY LOVE

1. *Think about the babies you've known or know now. Who was the person each first formed an attachment to? In what ways could you observe that attachment?*

Answers will vary.

2. *What does the Harlows' experiment with a terry-cloth "mother" teach us about childcare?*

It teaches us the importance of warm physical contact between a baby and its caretaker. It demonstrates that babies have a tremendous need to be held and cuddled, especially when they are frightened or unhappy. Caretakers should learn from this experiment that lovingly touching a baby is as important as feeding and changing it.

How does reading "Baby Love" affect your sense of what a baby needs?

3. *If you were the head of an orphanage, how might you use the information in "Baby Love" to benefit the children?*

"Baby Love" indicates that children need individual loving attention and physical closeness from their caregivers in order to develop normally. Children in orphanages could easily miss out on that kind of attention, since employees are likely to concentrate on supplying their physical needs, such as feeding and dressing them. The head of an orphanage could correct that by bringing in additional staff, either paid or volunteer, whose job it was to play with, hold, cuddle, and talk to individual babies and children.

Do you think it would be better to have paid employees or volunteers come in to cuddle and play with the children? Why?

4. *The authors write, "You may have doubts about generalizing to humans from experiments with monkeys." Then they go on to present two reasons why they feel the experiments on monkeys raise issues important to humans. Explain these reasons. Do you think they are good reasons? Why or why not?*

The reasons presented are (1) apes and monkeys are closely related to humans and share many traits with us, and (2) like the monkeys in the experiments, children who are brought up in isolation do develop social and emotional difficulties. Answers as to whether these are good reasons will vary.

Why do you think the experimenters concentrated on monkeys rather than human beings?

25

1. What is your reaction to this reading? Do its facts surprise you? Why or why not?

Answers will vary.

Before reading the selection, did you have an image of what family relationships in the old days might have been like?

2. The author writes that "when wives beat their husbands, it was the husband, not the wife, who was likely to be punished. . . . He had shamed the village by not controlling his wife properly." Do you think there are still men today who feel they are supposed to "control" their wives? Explain.

Answers will vary, but students should recognize that "control" can take many forms, from blatant physical control to more subtle emotional control.

3. In paragraph 7, Stark states that in the traditional family "the primary unit of society and attachment was not the family but the peer group." Does this statement apply at all to our society? At which stages or in what situations might people today feel closer to their peers than to their family members?

Teenagers are a group that is frequently strongly influenced by peers. For many teens, fitting into the social group is a more important need than almost anything else. People entering any new stage of life may look to their peers as examples. For instance, children beginning school, young people going away to college, or newlyweds might pay a lot of attention to their peer groups, because they are not sure of themselves in their new roles and believe the group can show them how they ought to behave.

At what points in your life have your peers been of special importance to you?

4. The author writes, "Only in modern times have most people married for love." Do you think love is the only thing people consider today when choosing a mate? What other factors might be important to consider when selecting a potential life partner?

The high divorce rate suggests that love alone is often not enough to make a good marriage. The ability of a couple to live together successfully depends on other factors as well, including their similar values regarding goals, having and raising children, managing conflict, handling finances, spending free time, planning for the future, and dividing up responsibilities in the marriage.

What are two or three points that you think will be especially important to you as you choose a spouse? (Or, if you are already married, what issues went into that decision for you?)

5 JULIA BURNEY: THE POWER OF A WOMAN'S DREAM

1. *Julia is passionate about the importance of reading. What is your attitude toward reading? Explain. Do you read much in your everyday life? If not, what kinds of reading do you think you might like to do more of?*

Answers will vary.

2. *The story implies that her parents' example kept Julia from experimenting with drugs, alcohol, or tobacco. On the basis of your observation, what is the most important influence on children when it comes to making a similar decision? Is it their parents' example, for better or worse? The behavior of peers? Or something else?*

Children can be influenced from many directions, and students' answers will depend upon their own observations. As Julia's experience shows, parents' examples play a big role in many children's lives. But many studies show that peers have at least as much influence on children's behavior. (That raises the related question of why children select the friends that they do. Why do some children gravitate toward friends who will be negative influences in their lives, while others prefer friends who will encourage them in positive directions?) What children see on TV, in movies, and through other media can also influence them. Or children may copy the behavior of an older role model whose example, positive or negative, appeals to them in some way.

3. *Julia credits her Aunt Ruby with encouraging her to love reading. She says that through her work with the Cops 'n Kids Center, she is repaying a debt to her aunt. As a child, did you have an adult in your life who provided a special kind of support and encouragement? Explain. What effect did that adult's actions have upon you?*

Answers will vary. If students do not immediately think of a special adult, encourage them to go a little more deeply into their memories. Young people often do remember a supportive person— a Sunday school teacher, local merchant, coach, parent's friend, etc.—with whom they had a warm, positive contact, even if it was fleeting in nature.

4. *How can adults most effectively encourage children to become readers? If you eventually have children yourself or are in contact with young children, what do you think you might do to encourage them to read?*

Some possible answers: Read age-appropriate books to a child from birth onward (starting with picture books). Make reading together a special part of the day, so the child starts to think of reading as a favorite activity. Make sure there is plenty of reading material available in the home. Buy the child his or her own books, and put them in the child's bedroom. Make sure the child observes his or her parents reading for pleasure. Limit exposure to TV and other electronic forms of entertainment. Make family trips to the library a regular event. Ask the child questions about what he or she is reading.

6 THE INFLUENCE OF THE SELF-FULFILLING PROPHECY

1. *In general, do you accept the premise of this reading: that our expectations have a great deal to do with what we later experience? What evidence have you seen that makes you agree or disagree with the author's premise?*

Answers will vary.

2. *Is it better to expect good things to happen, or to expect the worst and then be pleasantly surprised when things go well? Explain your answer.*

This question will divide the optimists and pessimists in the classroom. Optimists may say that we lose nothing by expecting good things to happen. Pessimists may call optimists unrealistic, pointing out that if we always expect the best, we aren't making alternative plans in case something bad happens.

3. *The authors write about people who are especially sensitive to rejection, and who seem to perceive it where it may not exist. Have you ever witnessed this happening? Why do you think it occurs?*

Probably everyone knows someone who is hypersensitive to rejection and who perceives rejection everywhere. Such people are usually unsure of their social skills. Their own nervousness and awkwardness may make others uncomfortable around them. At the first hint of other people's discomfort, they withdraw, feeling surer than ever that they've been "rejected."

4. *How might parents and teachers make use of what was demonstrated by* Pygmalion in the Classroom*?*

The *Pygmalion in the Classroom* experiment gives parents and teachers convincing evidence that children will rise, or fall, according to the expectations surrounding them. The lesson is clear: Parents and teachers should do all they can to communicate to kids that they believe the kids can be successful—and expect them to be successful.

1. *Sutherland describes several techniques she used to influence her husband. List these techniques and explain how each one develops her central point.*

Sutherland's central point is that people, like animals, can be "trained" to change their behaviors. Sutherland describes the technique called "approximations," which consists of rewarding small steps towards the desired behavior. By noticing and praising her husband's smallest advances toward a goal—throwing even one dirty sock into the hamper—she encouraged his progress.

A second technique is the development of "incompatible behaviors," meaning making the undesirable behavior impossible by replacing it with something else. Rather than express her irritation at the way her husband hovered around her as she made dinner, she made it impossible for him to hover by involving him in another task.

Finally, Sutherland describes "least reinforcing syndrome," a technique of not responding in any way to undesirable behavior. When her husband was looking for his keys, she completely ignored his growing irritation. By ignoring that behavior, she avoided "rewarding" him with any attention, even negative attention.

2. *Despite her lighthearted comparison of her husband, Scott, to an "exotic animal," Sutherland clearly loves and respects him. Where in the essay does she indicate her true feelings about her husband? Would you say that their marriage is a good one? Why or why not?*

Early in the essay, Sutherland describes her husband as well read, adventurous, and funny. At the end, when she realizes that he is using her techniques to train her, she recognizes her own less-than-perfect behavior. Generally, the marriage described seems to be a pretty healthy one, with ordinary squabbles. Have students point out specific evidence to back up their opinion that the marriage is good or not.

3. *In your opinion, was Sutherland justified in using animal-training techniques on her husband? Why or why not? How would you feel if you learned that someone was using similar techniques to "train" you?*

Answers will vary. Some students will find the idea of "training" a spouse offensive. The "trainer" can be viewed as a superior, more powerful being, while the "trained" can be seen as an inferior. But at the essay's end, when Scott begins to "train" Sutherland, students may feel that the balance of power has been restored.

4. *Have you ever tried to change the behavior of someone close to you? If so, what techniques did you use? Were they successful or unsuccessful? Would you be willing to try some of the techniques Sutherland has described in this essay?*

Answers will vary.

8   HARD TIMES, A HELPING HAND

1. *The author says that his mother never told him that his grandfather was the anonymous donor, B. Virdot. Why do you think she kept this information hidden from him? Would you also have kept the donor's identity secret? Why or why not?*

    Perhaps because "B. Virdot" hadn't wanted his identity made public, his family had gotten into the habit of keeping the story a secret. Answers to the second part of the question will vary. People might choose *not* to tell in order to protect the identity of the donor and maintain the privacy of those he helped. People might tell because they were proud of what "B. Virdot" had done and wanted to hold him up as an example to their children.

2. *If you were in a position to help others by giving them money, would you wish to remain anonymous, like the author's grandfather, or would you wish to be publicly acknowledged? What might be some drawbacks of your good deeds becoming known? Explain.*

    Being acknowledged for one's assistance could be gratifying. It might be nice to have people express their gratitude and praise one as a generous person. On the other hand, being publicly acknowledged might lead to more and more people asking for your help, or complaints that you had helped the "wrong" people in the "wrong" way.

3. *The author states that "Like many in his generation, my grandfather believed in hard work, and disdained handouts." Do you think the same holds true of the present generation? Or have Americans changed since the 1930s? Explain.*

    Answers will vary. There are conflicting widespread beliefs about Americans today: first, that they are overly dependent on welfare and other government programs; second, that with the loss of blue-collar jobs and the downturn in the economy, that they cannot expect to "pull themselves up by their bootstraps" without various forms of assistance.

4. *Ted Gup sees his grandfather as an example of how Americans reach out to one another in hard times. Do you know of anyone today who is reaching out to help others? If so, who is this person, and what is he or she doing to help others? Is what this person is doing something that other people could do as well? Explain.*

    Answers will vary. Encourage students to think of people who reach out in small, personal ways as well as large ways.

1. *Imagine that you were a subject in one of Milgram's experiments. How do you think you would have responded to the experimenter's commands? Why?*

Students need to ask themselves how much they are swayed by the commands of people in authority; whether they would assume they should complete their assignment or whether they would feel justified in withdrawing from the experiment.

2. *The authors write, "Presumably, obedience to legitimate authorities is something we learn early in life and retain throughout adulthood." Why do you think people develop an obedience to authority?*

When we are young, we naturally look to older, more experienced people to teach us the things we need to know in life. We are taught from babyhood on up to obey our parents, teachers, and other authority figures.

If you have children someday (or have them now), will you be a fairly lenient parent—or one who demands a good deal of obedience? Why?

3. *What might the authors have been thinking of when they wrote that Milgram's experiments "stand out as . . . a warning for our society"? Can you think of any events that reflect unwise obedience to authority?*

The authors mention two notorious examples: those of slaughter of the Jews by Nazi soldiers, and the mass suicide in Jonestown. Too often, children who are kidnapped, abused, and molested by adults do not fight back or reveal what has happened because they are convinced they must obey the adults involved. Otherwise honest people sometimes pretend not to notice unethical practices that their employers engage in, for fear of what will happen if they disobey the boss. People who are sexually harassed or exploited by their supervisors sometimes tolerate the behavior because of a sense of obedience to authority.

From your observations, would you say this sense of obedience to authority extends to groups of friends? Do members of the group tend to obey a leader within that group, even though he or she is their same age?

4. *The reading refers to what is negative about obedience to authority. What do you think might be the positive aspects of such obedience?*

A level of obedience is necessary for the survival of our species and the good of the community. Lack of obedience can lead to physical danger for the child, as well as chaotic conditions in the home and society.

Think of some scenarios at home, in school, or in the larger community, and imagine what would happen if obedience to authority was non-existent.

1. *Which of Verderber's five methods of dealing with conflict do you or people you know typically use? Give examples.*

Answers will vary.

2. *Why do you think Verderber regards discussion as "the most desirable means of dealing with conflict in a relationship"? And why might he feel that discussion "is often difficult to accomplish"?*

Discussion is desirable because it focuses on the actual problem, rather than on the personalities of the people involved, their history together, or their fear of conflict. It involves looking at the problem fairly and objectively and coming to mutual agreement about the best solution. Both parties come away from the decision understanding why it was made and feeling that it was made fairly. Discussion is difficult because it demands that both parties go into the decision with an open mind, not trying to use manipulation, guilt, hurt, anger, or sulkiness to bring about the decision they want. It is human nature to want to prove that one is "right" rather than genuinely be open to considering alternative solutions.

Do you know anyone who seems to be particularly good at using discussion to resolve conflicts? What do you observe about his or her technique?

3. *Verderber writes that conflict is sometimes useful because it forces us to make choices and test attitudes. When in your life has conflict been a good thing? What did you learn from it?*

Answers will vary.

4. *Suggest ways that someone you know could be encouraged to deal effectively with his or her specific conflict.*

Answers will vary.

SUGGESTED ANSWERS TO THE DISCUSSION QUESTIONS IN PART TWO

Note: For some questions, additional related questions have been included to enhance class discussion.

1 THE PROFESSOR IS A DROPOUT

1. *Lupe credits her fellow Hispanic students with being a great help to her in college. Is there anyone in your life—a teacher, family member, or friend—who has helped you through challenging times during your education? Explain what your obstacle was and how this person helped you to overcome it.*

   Answers will vary.

2. *Lupe found that her school responsibilities conflicted with her duties as wife and mother. What kinds of personal responsibilities have you had to juggle as a student? These may include parenthood, a job, a difficult home situation, extracurricular school activities, or anything else that poses a challenge to your academics. How have you balanced these obligations with your role as student?*

   Answers will vary.

3. *By the end of Lupe's story, we see the serious mistakes made by those who called her "retarded" and her children "slow learners." Was there ever a time when you felt people misjudged you? What did they say about you that was wrong, and how did it make you feel? Explain how you reacted to their judgments—did you accept their remarks, or did you fight to disprove them?*

   Answers will vary.

4. *Lupe is an outstanding example of a person who took charge of her life. Would you say that you have taken charge of your life? Describe how, or describe what you think you must yet do to take charge of your life.*

   Answers will vary. Encourage students to recognize even small accomplishments along the road to "taking control."

1. *What kinds of things make you most angry? Is your anger directed mostly at others, or at yourself? What steps do you think you should take, or what steps have you taken, to control anger?*

    Answers to the first two parts of the question will vary. In answering the final part, students might discuss such strategies as counting to ten before they speak, trying to put themselves in the other person's place, employing a sense of humor, or walking away from an anger-producing situation.

2. *If you were teaching a class to students on what they should do to control anger, what would be your advice?*

    Students may suggest any of the techniques mentioned in the answer to question 1. They might also suggest that displays of anger are often counterproductive and even harmful, or that while an angry outburst may make a person feel briefly better, the person often feels ashamed or embarrassed later.

3. *Of the three sources of our anger identified in the reading—time, technology, and tension—which do you think is the greatest problem for you? Why?*

    Answers will vary.

4. *Do you agree with Carol Tavris, author of* Anger: The Misunderstood Emotion, *that almost no situation is improved by an angry outburst? Is anger ever helpful? Explain your answer.*

    Some students may agree with Tavris that angry outbursts are never appropriate. Others may disagree, saying that it is dishonest, unhealthy, or counterproductive always to suppress one's anger. Students may cite situations in which a person does something hurtful or offensive and say that they feel the need to "stand up and be counted" by showing their anger.

1. *Kellmayer writes, "By 1944, the social climate had become more accepting of integration, in large part because of the contribution of black soldiers in World War II." Why do you think the contribution of black soldiers in World War II would be such an influence on the progress of integration in the United States?*

World War II was a popular war, supported by the great majority of Americans. The soldiers who fought and died in it were regarded as heroes. Many of those soldiers were black. The realizations that black and white soldiers had fought side by side for the same cause, and that black soldiers had been American war heroes, were powerful ones for many white Americans, forcing them to re-evaluate their thinking on racial issues after the war was over.

2. *An ongoing question about history is whether individuals cause important changes in society or whether it is circumstances that lead to changes—once the circumstances are right, the right individuals will emerge. In the integration of baseball, how important do you think the times were? How important were the individuals involved?*

Branch Rickey and Jackie Robinson were remarkable individuals whose dreams, drive, and talent are undeniable. But chances are good that those individuals could not have accomplished what they did a generation earlier. By the late 1940s, the contribution of black soldiers during World War II had given a huge boost to the growing sense that racial segregation could not survive in a democracy. Even under those circumstances, Robinson and the Dodgers faced enormous obstacles as the first integrated team. It is difficult to imagine that any individuals, no matter how gifted, could have made an integrated team succeed earlier.

3. *Do you think Branch Rickey was right to make Robinson agree "not to fight back"? Explain your answer.*

Students may object to Robinson's pacifism as a sign of weakness, or as giving in to Rickey's desire to show Robinson as a "good Negro." They may believe that Robinson's right to defend himself outweighed Rickey's wishes. Alternatively, they may look at the outcome of Robinson's actions and defend his restraint as having been justified. They may point out that if Robinson had fought back, his actions, rather than the integration of the team, would have become the focus of attention.

How do you think the Jackie Robinson/integration of baseball story would have been changed if Robinson had fought back against his tormenters?

4. *Robinson had to face a great deal of racism. Unfortunately, despite the greater integration of today, racism still exists. Have you experienced any racial insults yourself or seen anyone else treated badly because of the racial or ethnic group he or she belongs to? Tell what happened, and how you or the other person reacted.*

Answers will vary.

1. Why do you think that Worthington and his mother were unable to persuade Worthington's father to try to learn to read and write? Can you think of anything they could have done that might have had better results?

Worthington's father was deeply embarrassed that he couldn't read. He was clearly a proud man who wanted to take good care of his family. It was probably very difficult for him to let his wife and son witness just how helpless he was in that area. Possibly if he could have worked with a tutor who was skilled in teaching adults to read, he might have felt less embarrassed and more able to learn.

2. Worthington's father's first experience of learning to read was a bad one. Were your earliest experiences of learning to read generally positive—or negative? What made them so? Do you think these early experiences have influenced your present attitude toward reading? Explain.

Answers will vary. Encourage students to share their memories of who they were reading with, where those experiences took place, and what they were reading.

3. How have attitudes toward people with learning disabilities changed since Worthington's father's time? Overall, do you think today's teachers are more helpful toward students who find reading difficult? Or is our educational system still failing them?

There is more recognition than there was in Worthington's father's time that people learn differently, and more recognition of learning disabilities such as dyslexia that can interfere with a person's learning. Many schools have special help available for students who struggle with reading. On the other hand, many schools are overcrowded and understaffed, and children who do not read well can easily slip through the cracks and be promoted despite their poor reading skills.

4. In your opinion, is illiteracy still a major problem in the United States? What evidence can you give for your answer? If you knew someone who you suspected might be illiterate, what could you do to help him or her?

Answers will vary. Students could help an illiterate person by helping him or her find a tutor or program. Encourage your students to be aware of programs, such as the National Institute for Literacy, which can direct people to literacy programs in their area. Local libraries are often good places to start to find literacy tutors.

5 MOTIVATION AND NEEDS

1. *Do you know a workaholic, a compulsive gambler, a television addict, or a joiner? Which of Maslow's needs do you think each of these people is trying to meet?*

Workaholics and gamblers may both be motivated by the need to achieve. However, workaholics seek personal accomplishments, while gamblers may seek achievement through luck. A person may be addicted to television as a means of fulfilling his or her stimulation needs; or perhaps a television addict fears success, and uses TV partly to avoid real-world challenges. Finally, a joiner may seek to fulfill his or her affiliation needs.

2. *What ads have you seen recently that appeal to our need for approval? Which ones begin with a "negative appeal," as Quinn describes it in paragraph 18?*

Answers will vary, but the following guidelines may help:

- "Bandwagon" advertisements appeal to our desire to belong to a group. Ads that use this appeal imply that if we use the sponsor's product, we will be "jumping on the bandwagon."

- In addition, many ads for cosmetics and toiletries appeal to the desire to look and smell good—qualities intended to make us more lovable. Some ads show a "before and after" scenario in which someone is first shown negatively, then wins approval, popularity, even romance after using the product.

3. *On the basis of your own experience, why might some people fear success? And what reasons can you see for the fear of success being much more common among women than among men?*

As Quinn points out (paragraph 27), fear of success usually stems from the need for love and belongingness. Some younger students associate academic success with peer rejection—the "it's not cool to do well in school" syndrome. Similar feelings may cause workers to hold back on the job, fearful that their higher productivity, for example, especially if publicly recognized by the boss, might earn the resentment and disapproval of their colleagues. Women's fear of success could be due to a number of factors: the so-called "feminine" outlook that fosters cooperation over competition; the desire for approbation based (traditionally) on their appearance and social skills, not their achievements; the reluctance to appear too "masculine" by pursuing external, real-world goals; and the reluctance to compete and win against men, influenced by the childhood lesson that "boys don't like girls who beat them."

4. *According to the reading, achievements are a key way to satisfy the need for esteem and self-esteem. What achievements of yours have most strengthened your esteem and self-esteem? What achievement goals do you have for the future?*

Answers will vary, but students may wish to share their skills and talents with the class and the achievements those abilities have helped them both reach and aim for.

6 EFFECTS OF THE AUTOMOBILE

1. *The author lists numerous effects of the automobile, but does he think any of those effects are positive or negative? Look at the reading and try to determine the author's opinion of the various effects he describes.*

As the author describes how the automobile allowed people to leave the cities for the suburbs, and allowed farmers to travel easily from their villages to the city, he seems to suggest that the breakdown of the cities and "drying up" of the villages was a negative consequence.

An automobile-related change that the author seems to see as positive is the changed role of women in society. He notes that before the automobile, women were largely confined to their homes, making few decisions and having little independence. With the increased freedom that the cars provided, "[women] gained greater control over the family budget, and as their horizons extended beyond the confines of their home, they also gained different views of life."

The other effects the author describes seem to be ones he views in more neutral terms—as neither especially positive or especially negative.

2. *Most people's lives would be different without the automobile and its automotive "relatives," such as the van, truck, bus, tractor, and motorcycle. How would your life change if there were suddenly no automobiles?*

Answers will vary.

3. *The selection explains that domestic chores were greatly changed with the introduction of the car and the electric refrigerator. Give some examples of other technological inventions that have changed domestic chores.*

Electrical appliances such as the vacuum cleaner, stove, freezer, washing machine, toaster, microwave oven, and dishwasher have all affected domestic life. The telephone and computer both make at-home shopping a reality.

What invention has had the greatest impact on your domestic life?

4. *The passage argues that the automobile stands out as a candidate for the "single item that has had the greatest impact on social life in the twentieth century." Can you think of another item that has also had—or will have—a tremendous impact on society? What is it, and what are some of its more important effects?*

Some candidates for "most important item" include the telephone, the TV, and the personal computer. The telephone—along with its offspring, the cell phone and "smartphone"—allows instantaneous voice and, now, visual communication between all corners of the world. TV has had immeasurable influence because it keeps viewers informed of changes in their world; because popular programs influence our tastes, thoughts, and topics of conversation; and because watching TV has changed the ways families spend time together. The ultimate effect of the personal computer can only be guessed at as yet, but the vast storehouse of information, entertainment, shopping options, and social interaction it puts at a user's fingertips is sure to have an even greater impact on future generations.

What are the drawbacks, if any, of the item you think of as "most important"? What negative effects has it had on society?

1. *The tone of this essay can best be described as objective. Why has the author chosen to treat the subject matter in such a way?*

The purpose of a medical reference book is to inform in a straightforward fashion, not to entertain, alarm, or persuade. More dramatic or exciting discussions of rabies are available, but they would not do as effective a job of simply presenting useful information.

2. *According to the article, many of the animals people typically associate with rabies—rats, mice, and other small mammals—rarely carry the disease. Have you ever had an idea about a disease, or a treatment for a disease, that you discovered to be false? Explain. What do you think causes people to believe false ideas?*

Answers will vary. False, unproven, or exaggerated ideas about diseases are common (for instance, that leprosy is highly contagious, that wearing a copper bracelet will relieve arthritis, that a poison ivy rash can spread from one person to another, that colds or even pneumonia are caused by getting one's feet wet). Because the causes of disease are generally not visible to the naked eye, people from the beginning of time have looked for explanations for them. In an attempt to gain a sense of control over our bodies and health, we are willing to believe theories and treatments that are not necessarily factual.

3. *This essay appears in a current medical reference book designed for home use. Do you have such a medical reference book at home? How do you typically get medical information when you need it?*

Answers will vary. Many resources are available for getting medical information: one's own doctor, friends and family members, encyclopedias and other reference books, publications available at clinics and other public places, health hotlines listed in the telephone book, health-related TV and radio shows, and the Internet.

How do you distinguish between dependable medical information and medical information (or, for that matter, any information) that may be false?

4. *A major section of this essay concerns prevention. When did you become aware of the value of preventive medicine? What steps, if any, do you take in your daily life to prevent general health problems? If you are not currently doing anything to prevent illness, what could you begin doing to protect yourself?*

Answers will vary. A few common means people use to prevent health problems:

- Eat a healthful diet
- Take vitamins
- Exercise daily
- Stop smoking
- Don't drink excessively
- Practice safe sex
- Monitor known health problems (such as high blood pressure or diabetes) and follow doctor's orders

8 BAD MANAGERS

1. *Describe the worst boss you ever had. Which of the behaviors described in this selection did your boss exhibit? How did those behaviors affect you and other employees?*

   Answers will vary.

2. *The reading describes problem managers but gives no advice on how workers should deal with them. Select one of the incompetent or malicious managers described in the reading. What advice would you give to someone who was trying to deal with such a boss?*

   As the article says, bad managers are often poor because they are driven by fear: fear that they will make the wrong decision, that they'll look foolish, that they'll have to go out on a limb. In order to deal with such a manager (or any difficult person), it can be helpful to put oneself in his or her shoes and figure out how to relieve that fear. An employee who learns to understand and work around a manager's fear may have more success dealing with him or her. Eventually, of course, a employee may have to accept the fact that a manager is too much trouble to deal with and start looking for another job.

3. *On the basis of the information in this article and your own experience, describe the qualities of a person you would consider an ideal boss.*

   Answers will vary. This article makes it clear that a common characteristic of a poor boss is refusal to take responsibility for decision-making. It can be assumed, then, that a willingness to make decisions is a desirable quality in a manager. Good humor, fairness, consistency, and the willingness to give recognition and praise are other qualities that many people would mention as highly desirable in a boss.

4. *What steps do you think companies should take to protect employees from incompetent or malicious bosses?*

   It would be helpful if a company had clearly stated channels for an employee to go through when he or she had a complaint. For instance, a company might encourage workers to report problems to the board of directors or the human resources director—in other words, to someone who is not under the supervision of the manager who is being complained about.

1. Do you have a pet? If so, how inactive is that animal? What do you think might be the similarities and differences between your pet's needs and the needs of animals living in the wild?

Answers will vary. In general, all animals have the same needs. However, pets have nearly all of these needs provided for them by their owners. For example, pets are not affected by seasonal changes nearly as much as animals in the wild are. Many wild animals must store food for the cold winter months; pets do not have this need. Further, wild animals must adapt in physical appearance for survival. For example, during the winter months, their fur often becomes thicker. As a result of these differences, it is not as much a matter of survival for pets to be inactive as it is for wild animals.

2. The article mentions that some scientists object to the term "laziness" being applied to animals and insects. The concept of laziness may apply only to humans. Can you think of any other human characteristics that are frequently attributed to animals? Do you believe the animals actually have those characteristics?

Answers will vary. There are a number of human characteristics that are frequently attributed to animals. Probably most common among these is human emotions. Humans tend to believe their pets are jealous, angry, or lonely, when the humans themselves may actually be experiencing these emotions. Yet it is often said that only a pet can offer a human unconditional love.

3. In writing about the animal researchers and their work, the author could have used a formal, scientific tone or a lighter, more informal approach. Which tone did she use, and why do you think she made that choice? Find examples to support your opinion.

Angier uses a light, informal tone in this selection. This tone makes the article accessible to everyone, not just those in the science fields. It also changes what might have been a very dry subject to one that is vivid and interesting.

    Some examples of Angier's informal tone include the following excerpts:

- "So while there may not be a specific gene for laziness, there is always a good excuse."
- The heading "Flying Is So Draining"
- "Some species . . . fulfill the occasional social obligation, like picking fleas from a fellow creature's fur."

4. Books, articles, and television shows about animal behavior are often very popular. How would you explain the fascination that animal behavior holds for people?

One reason humans may be fascinated by animal behavior is that there seem to be two sides to animals. When animals are pets, we tend to view them as having "human" emotions and characteristics. We often think of our pets as gentle, kind, or mild-mannered. It is intriguing, then, to see animals in the wild, where survival is proportional to strength.

1. *How does Savory's attitude toward homosexuality change in the course of the selection? What incident marks the turning point in her attitude toward her own sexuality?*

For years, Savory was unhappy, ashamed, and confused about her sexuality. Her attitude changes after she reads the angry article that claims homosexuality is a choice. In her confusion and pain, she decides that she will "choose" to be straight. But when she tells her father of her decision, he gently encourages her to see that she would only be pretending in order to make other people think she was straight. His acceptance of her gayness gave her comfort and courage.

2. *What comparison does Savory draw between the treatment of blacks and the treatment of gays? In your view, is this comparison convincing? Explain.*

Savory suggests that both groups have been unfairly discriminated against and treated as second-class citizens. She points out that just as gays have been forbidden to marry one another, blacks and whites were also forbidden to marry. Answers to the second part of the question will vary.

3. *What did Savory feel was so unjust about the story of Sarah and Laura? If you agree with her attitude toward the couple, what steps could be taken to make sure that unfortunate situations like these no longer occur?*

Despite Sarah and Laura's long relationship, which was like a marriage, Sarah had no legal rights as Laura's spouse when Laura died. Sarah was not considered Laura's family and could not even visit her in the hospital. Instead, a blood relative of Laura's who had no personal relationship with her inherited her house and belongings.

If gay marriage is made legal, gay partners will have the same legal rights as straight married people. Unless a person directs otherwise in his or her will, a spouse automatically inherits a person's estate.

4. *In paragraph 28, Savory states that there will come a day when no one will really care one way or the other about sexual orientation. Do you agree or disagree with her belief? Explain.*

Answers will vary. Encourage students to explain what evidence they have for their answer.

MODEL NOTES AND ACTIVITIES
FOR "FOUR ADDITIONAL READINGS"

Comments and Suggestions

- This section contains the following for each of the four additional reading selections on pages 655–662 of the text:

    1. An outlining, mapping, or summarizing activity.
    2. The completed outline, map, or summary of the reading. These activities can be copied and distributed for comparison purposes after students have completed the activity or taken their own notes.

- The four readings can be assigned one at a time throughout the semester after students have worked through "Supporting Details," Chapter 3 in Part One, in which outlining, mapping, and summarizing are explained.

- I suggest assigning the readings in terms of level of difficulty. From easiest to hardest, I would sequence the readings as follows:

    Labeling and the Onset of Old Age *(easiest)*
    Nonverbal Communication
    Why Do Most Mothers Cradle Their Babies in Their Left Arms?
    Is Aggression a Response to Frustration? *(hardest)*

- Following are some notetaking guidelines you may wish to copy and pass out and/or briefly go over with students.

Some Notetaking Guidelines

- Before beginning to take notes, carefully read through and mark the material.

- Here's how to mark material: Circle definitions, set off examples with an *Ex,* and underline or bracket ideas that seem especially important. Use numbers (1, 2, 3 . . .) to mark off major items in a series.

- Then take notes by writing down each heading in turn and listing the important ideas that you find under that heading. Think carefully about each heading; it is often a key to main ideas and major details.

- Keep outlines simple. Often just one level of symbols (1, 2, 3 . . .) will do.

- Sometimes you may want two levels, and they can be labeled as follows:

  1.
      a.
      b.
  2.
      a.
      b.

- If you need three levels, they can be labeled as follows:

  A.
      1.
          a.
          b.
      2.
          a.
          b.
  B.
      1.
          a.
          b.
      2.
          a.
          b.
  etc.

OUTLINING ACTIVITY: "WHY DO MOST MOTHERS CRADLE THEIR BABIES IN THEIR LEFT ARMS?"

Complete the following outline of the selection.

Why do mothers cradle babies in left arm?

1. Obvious explanation: _____

    _____

    However:

    a. 78 percent of left-handed mothers also favor holding babies on left.
    b. 84 percent of chimpanzees and 83 percent of gorillas, who are not predominantly right-handed, also hold babies on left side.

2. Most likely reason: _____

    _____

    a. Baby heard sound while in womb; associates it with peace, comfort, security.
    b. In an experiment, babies who heard recorded sound of heartbeat fell asleep twice as quickly as those who did not.

3. Another possible reason: _____

    _____

    a. Emotions are more strongly expressed on left side of face; mother gives baby a better chance to read her mood changes.
    b. Mother's left eye and ear are more tuned in to baby's emotional changes than her right eye and ear would be.

4. A fourth possible reason: _____

    _____

    a. 70 percent of newborns enter the world with a preprogrammed tendency to turn their heads to the right.
    b. Mothers about to feed their babies find babies' heads turned to right, so a mother will hold her baby in her left arm so they can be "face to face."

AN OUTLINE OF "WHY DO MOST MOTHERS CRADLE THEIR BABIES IN THEIR LEFT ARMS?"

Why do mothers cradle babies in left arm?

1. Obvious explanation: Majority of mothers are right-handed and want to keep right hand free.

   However:

   a. 78 percent of left-handed mothers also favor holding babies on left.

   b. 84 percent of chimpanzees and 83 percent of gorillas, who are not predominantly right-handed, also hold babies on left side.

2. Most likely reason: Mothers are bringing infants closer to sound of heartbeat.

   a. Baby heard sound while in womb; associates it with peace, comfort, security.

   b. In an experiment, babies who heard recorded sound of heartbeat fell asleep twice as quickly as those who did not.

3. Another possible reason: Mother is showing baby her "best side."

   a. Emotions are more strongly expressed on left side of face; mother gives baby a better chance to read her mood changes.

   b. Mother's left eye and ear are more tuned in to baby's emotional changes than her right eye and ear would be.

4. A fourth possible reason: The baby, not the mother, is responsible for the preference.

   a. 70 percent of newborns enter the world with a preprogrammed tendency to turn their heads to the right.

   b. Mothers about to feed their babies find babies' heads turned to right, so a mother will hold her baby in her left arm so they can be "face to face."

MAPPING ACTIVITY: "LABELING AND THE ONSET OF OLD AGE"

1. _____

_____

Ex.— wrinkles, balding, aches, difficulty in doing things that used to be taken for granted

2. _____

_____

Ex.— an accident, early motherhood or grandmotherhood

There are several factors that make people label themselves as "old."

3. _____

_____

Def.— _____

_____

_____

Ex.— _____

_____

_____

Ex.— U.S. television: older male news anchors are retained; older female anchors are not

Ex.— In movies, older men more likely to play romantic leads opposite much younger female stars

4. _____

_____

Def.— _____

_____

_____

Ex.— _____

_____

_____

A MAP OF "LABELING AND THE ONSET OF OLD AGE"

1. Biology

Ex.—wrinkles, balding, aches, difficulty in doing things that used to be taken for granted

2. Personal history or biography

Ex.—an accident, early motherhood or grandmotherhood

There are several factors that make people label themselves as "old."

3. Gender age

Def.— the relative value that a culture places on men's and women's ages

Ex.— On men, graying hair and wrinkles are signs of "maturing"; on women, they are signs of being old

Ex.— U.S. television: older male news anchors are retained; older female anchors are not

Ex.— In movies, older men more likely to play romantic leads opposite much younger female stars

4. Timetables

Def.— signals that societies use to inform their members they are old

Ex.— a particular birthday, the inability to perform productive social roles

OUTLINING ACTIVITY: "NONVERBAL COMMUNICATION"

A. Importance of nonverbal communication

    1. Accounts for 55 percent of our total communication.

    2. When verbal and nonverbal communication conflict, people believe nonverbal.

    3. _____

        a. If a coworker gives you an unusual glance, you wonder what it meant.

        b. Some employees avoid greeting others and instead show "frozen faces," which can be interpreted as displeasure.

        c. Some body language can be misleading: crossed arms may not mean lack of receptivity—only that the person feels cold.

B. _____

    1. Accenting: _____

        a. Poking finger into someone's chest

        b. _____

    2. _____: reinforcing verbal communication

        a. _____

        b. Standing four feet away from your boss and saluting her formally reinforces the message that she is of higher rank and has unchallenged authority.

    3. _____

        a. Often this is how people reveal true feelings or send an unintended message.

        b. For example, _____

        c. When verbal and nonverbal messages conflict, people believe the nonverbal ones.

    4. _____

        a. _____

        b. Tapping a coworker's shoulder while she is walking away means you want her to stop or wait for you.

        c. _____

    5. _____

        a. _____

        b. _____

AN OUTLINE OF "NONVERBAL COMMUNICATION"

A. Importance of nonverbal communication
   1. Accounts for 55 percent of our total communication.
   2. When verbal and nonverbal communication conflict, people believe nonverbal.
   3. Every gesture or glance communicates a message.
      a. If a coworker gives you an unusual glance, you wonder what it meant.
      b. Some employees avoid greeting others and instead show "frozen faces," which can be interpreted as displeasure.
      c. Some body language can be misleading: crossed arms may not mean lack of receptivity—only that the person feels cold.

B. Functions of nonverbal communication
   1. Accenting: punctuating verbal communication
      a. Poking finger into someone's chest
      b. Sweeping motion of hand to say that conversation is over

   2. Complementing: reinforcing verbal communication
      a. Standing four feet away from someone might indicate the person is a stranger.
      b. Standing four feet away from your boss and saluting her formally reinforces the message that she is of higher rank and has unchallenged authority.

   3. Contradicting: conveying messages opposite to the verbal messages
      a. Often this is how people reveal true feelings or send an unintended message.
      b. For example, people who give less eye contact than they receive send the message that they are bored.
      c. When verbal and nonverbal messages conflict, people believe the nonverbal ones.

   4. Regulating: controlling the course of a conversation
      a. Raising a hand with index finger extended means you want the other person to wait or to stop speaking.
      b. Tapping a coworker's shoulder while she is walking away means you want her to stop or wait for you.
      c. Touching someone's arm while he speaks means you want to speak.

   5. Substituting: replacing the verbal messages
      a. When we're in a hurry, we raise both eyebrows instead of asking how somebody is doing.
      b. We shake our heads while standing behind the boss to show we don't agree with what he is saying.

SUMMARIZING ACTIVITY:
"IS AGGRESSION A RESPONSE TO FRUSTRATION?"

Study notes:

Original frustration-aggression theory: _____

_____

_____

Frustration — anything that blocks _____

Displacement — _____

    Ex. — _____

_____

_____

Revised frustration-aggression theory: _____

_____

_____

One kind of aggressive cue — _____

_____

    Ex. — _____

_____

_____

Ex. — Countries that ban handguns have lower murder rates. (The United States has about 10,000 handgun homicides per year; Britain has about 10.)

A SUMMARY OF
"IS AGGRESSION A RESPONSE TO FRUSTRATION?"

Study notes:

Original frustration-aggression theory: frustration always leads to some form of aggression, although the aggression need not be directed against the source of the frustration.

Frustration — anything that blocks our attaining a goal

Displacement — redirecting our aggression toward safer targets

Ex. — A man who is humiliated by his boss takes it out on his wife; she yells at their son; the son kicks the dog; the dog bites the mail carrier.

Revised frustration-aggression theory: frustration produces anger, an emotional readiness to aggress, which is especially likely to explode when aggressive cues are present.

One kind of aggressive cue — the sight of a weapon perceived as an instrument of violence

Ex. — Children who had just played with toy guns were more than willing to knock down another child's blocks.

Ex. — Countries that ban handguns have lower murder rates. (The United States has about 10,000 handgun homicides per year; Britain has about 10.)

TEST BANK

This section contains the following:

- A **Test Bank** (pages 55–142) consisting of four additional mastery tests for each chapter in Part One of *Ten Steps to Advancing College Reading Skills*, Fifth Edition, as well as four additional Combined-Skills Mastery Tests;
- An **answer key** (pages 143–146) to the 44 tests in the test bank.

Instructors whose students are using *Ten Steps to Advancing College Reading Skills*, Fifth Edition, in class have permission to reproduce any of these tests on a photocopying machine (or a secure website) as often as needed.

VOCABULARY IN CONTEXT: Test A

A. For each item below, underline the **examples** that suggest the meaning of the italicized term. Then, in the space provided, write the letter of the meaning of that term.

___ 1. Duane is the *antithesis* of his brother. For instance, Duane is very shy while his brother is outgoing. Also, Duane enjoys reading while his brother prefers playing sports.
  A. opposite   C. enemy
  B. imitation   D. hero

___ 2. Our neighbor has an *abrasive* personality. He can't seem to get along with people without frequent outbursts and quarrels.
  A. quiet and sweet   C. analytical
  B. cool   D. harsh and rough

B. Each item below includes a word or words that are a **synonym** of the italicized word. Write the synonym of the italicized word in the space provided.

_____ 3. Some actors are as *adroit* in business as they are skilled in performing.

_____ 4. Marie is a *meticulous* worker, but it's no surprise—her mother is also extremely careful and precise.

_____ 5. The mayor and the governor feel the same about each other—he *deplores* her as much as she disapproves of him.

C. Each item below includes a word or words that are an **antonym** of the italicized word. Underline the antonym of each italicized word. Then write the letter of the meaning of the italicized word.

___ 6. Jo left her term paper till the last minute and was able to do only *cursory* research. In contrast, Ian started his paper in plenty of time; his painstaking, thorough research earned him an A.
  A. hasty   C. careful
  B. rude   D. indirect

___ 7. Nina makes a big fuss about every little thing her children do, whether it's harmful or *innocuous*.
  A. loud   C. dangerous
  B. stubborn   D. harmless

(Continues on next page)

D. Use the **general sense of each sentence** to figure out the meaning of each italicized word. Then write the letter of the meaning of the italicized word.

___ 8. My old dented car looks *incongruous* among my neighbors' fancy new cars.
    A. useful
    B. appropriate
    C. better
    D. out of place

___ 9. It isn't *feasible* for me to attend the 12:30 meeting—I've got another important meeting that begins at noon.
    A. correct
    B. possible
    C. noticeable
    D. difficult

___10. It is usually obvious when someone has an *egocentric* personality. Ms. A., for instance, can talk of nothing but herself, and Mr. B. has no interest in anything that doesn't affect him directly.
    A. careless
    B. violent
    C. caring
    D. self-centered

VOCABULARY IN CONTEXT: Test B

A. For each item below, underline the **examples** that suggest the meaning of the italicized term. Then, in the space provided, write the letter of the meaning of that term.

____ 1. To cheer up the hallway, Reba *embellished* her children's bedroom doors. She painted colorful circus pictures on her son's door and pasted seashells on her daughter's.

    A. replaced   C. decorated
    B. erased   D. recognized

____ 2. People in *sedentary* occupations, such as driving a taxi or writing books, need to make a special effort to exercise.

    A. high-stress   C. involving much sitting
    B. very well-paid   D. artistic

____ 3. My grandfather says that his teachers had students do *inane* things, such as spending hours on improving handwriting and memorizing the date each of the fifty states entered the union.

    A. wise   C. impossible
    B. foolish   D. expensive

B. Each item below includes a word or words that are a **synonym** of the italicized word. Write the synonym of the italicized word in the space provided.

_____ 4. Raheem has a *belligerent* nature. His friends can't explain why he faces the world with such a hostile attitude.

_____ 5. The houses along the river are in a *precarious* position, so they are often flooded. Yet afterward, the owners keep stubbornly rebuilding on the same risky sites.

C. Each item below includes a word or words that are an **antonym** of the italicized word. Underline the antonym of each italicized word. Then write the letter of the meaning of the italicized word.

____ 6. Ling is not self-praising, like her brother; in fact, she's self-*disparaging*.

    A. encouraging   C. knowing
    B. belittling   D. appealing

____ 7. On television, a speech may seem *impromptu* even though it's prepared. Speakers can read from a script that the audience cannot see.

    A. controversial   C. dull
    B. overly long   D. unrehearsed

(Continues on next page)

D. Use the **general sense of each sentence** to figure out the meaning of each italicized word. Then write the letter of the meaning of the italicized word.

___ 8. Unhappy with British rule, the American colonists fought to become *autonomous*.
   A. well-known
   B. taxed
   C. independent
   D. reasonable

___ 9. Our state representative *disseminates* useful information to residents in her district through letters, local interviews, and e-mail.
   A. collects
   B. believes
   C. distributes
   D. prevents

___ 10. Late for work because of a subway breakdown, Sean was afraid the boss wouldn't believe him. He was relieved when six coworkers came forward to *corroborate* his excuse.
   A. support
   B. listen to
   C. contradict
   D. ask for

VOCABULARY IN CONTEXT: Test C

Using context clues for help, write the letter of the best meaning for each italicized word or words.

____ 1. No one knows how humans acquired the concept of cooking food, but their first experience of cooking was probably *fortuitous:* very likely, some meat fell into a fire by accident.
   A. harmful
   B. planned
   C. lucky
   D. expensive

____ 2. Many husbands still find it difficult to *render* total support to their wives' careers, particularly if their wives earn more than they do.
   A. cook
   B. hide
   C. give
   D. delay

____ 3. The Amazonian forest in Brazil is so *expansive* that it influences weather and climate patterns.
   A. far
   B. huge
   C. green
   D. mysterious

____ 4. In the early 1900s, sums paid to widows with dependent children were *meager,* ranging from $2 to $14 a month for the first child and lesser amounts for the rest.
   A. inadequate
   B. old-fashioned
   C. harmful
   D. generous

____ 5. Running a *clandestine* operation—such as an underground newspaper in a dictatorship, a network of spies, or an undercover police investigation—is difficult and often highly dangerous.
   A. important
   B. expensive
   C. legal
   D. secret

____ 6. Good communication between marriage partners can often *mitigate* the stress caused by physical signs of aging, changes in work status or satisfaction, or the death of close relatives and friends.
   A. lessen
   B. hide
   C. cause
   D. add to

____ 7. Identifying the age of layers of rock also *fixes* the age of fossils that are within those layers.
   A. causes
   B. hides
   C. establishes
   D. casts doubt on

(Continues on next page)

___ 8. Government *entails* those political processes that have to do with the forming of rules and policies which are binding throughout a society.
   A. includes
   B. recognizes
   C. outlaws
   D. omits

___ 9. The elephant was deeply *enmeshed* in the fabric of Thai life. For centuries, it served as Thailand's main mode of transportation; its image graced temples, palaces, and the national flag.
   A. hidden
   B. harmed
   C. involved
   D. weakened

___10. When we interact, we behave like actors by following a script that we have learned. When someone enters a doctor's waiting room, for instance, he or she *assumes* the role of patient.
   A. meets
   B. contacts
   C. denies
   D. takes on

VOCABULARY IN CONTEXT: Test D

Using context clues for help, write the letter of the best meaning for each italicized word or words.

____ 1. In addition to getting a jail sentence, some criminals are required to pay *restitution.* One thief had to pay an elderly woman both the money he stole from her and several thousand dollars for her injuries.

    A. a small fine   C. taxes

    B. payment to charity   D. repayment for loss

____ 2. In China, if you visit an acquaintance on a hot day and feel thirsty, you would not ask your host *point-blank,* "May I have a glass of water?" Instead, you would convey the same request by saying, "Isn't it hot today?"

    A. angrily   C. frequently

    B. directly   D. softly

____ 3. Measurement of population growth depends in large part on birth rates and *mortality* rates.

    A. marriage   C. death

    B. financial   D. education

____ 4. Contact, support, and encouragement between adult children and their parents are seldom one-way but are instead *reciprocal* interactions.

    A. selfish   C. give-and-take

    B. frequent   D. rare

____ 5. The Big Room at Carlsbad Caverns has an area equivalent to fourteen football fields and enough height to *accommodate* the U.S. Capitol Building.

    A. duplicate   C. easily reach

    B. find   D. contain

____ 6. There are many things about the campus library that make it *conducive* to studying, including good lighting, quiet, and nearby reference books.

    A. helpful   C. unattractive

    B. interesting   D. harmful

____ 7. Why do we use *platitudes?* One theory is that remarks such as "Nice to see you," "Have a good day," and "Take care" save us the trouble of having to think of what to say.

    A. sad comments   C. questions

    B. commonplace remarks   D. reasons

(Continues on next page)

_____ 8. "Quality circles" are small groups of employees that work together as equals. Practically all the companies that have *implemented* quality circles are in the manufacturing sector of the economy. Giving workers more control over their jobs can boost worker productivity.

    A. defined   C. seen often

    B. manufactured   D. put into effect

_____ 9. During the 1920s, advertising agencies hired psychologists to design the first ad campaigns. They *touted* products by building up name-brand identification, creating memorable slogans, manipulating endorsements by doctors or celebrities, and appealing to consumers' hunger for prestige and status.

    A. manufactured   C. bought

    B. named   D. promoted

_____ 10. In 1974, a Senate committee investigating the role of the Nixon administration in the Watergate break-in learned that President Nixon had made tape recordings of conversations with his advisors. When the special prosecutor demanded the tapes, Nixon refused, *invoking* executive privilege. He insisted that a president had a right to keep confidential any White House communication.

    A. referring to for support   C. forgetting

    B. causing   D. fighting against

MAIN IDEAS: Test A

The following paragraphs have main ideas that may appear at various places within the paragraph. Identify the topic sentence of each paragraph by filling in the correct sentence number in the space provided.

____ 1. ¹Not that many decades ago, the entertainment world had a history of discrimination against black performers. ²For many years, for instance, radio listeners tuned in to *Amos 'n' Andy,* a popular situation comedy about two black men. ³But the actors who played Amos and Andy were both white. ⁴In those same years, before the start of the civil rights movement, talented black singers were hired to dub in movie songs for white actresses who couldn't sing. ⁵The singers' names, however, could never appear in the movie credits.

____ 2. ¹Actors are nervous before a play. ²Politicians are nervous before they give a campaign speech. ³Athletes are nervous before a big game. ⁴Surveys show that 76 percent of experienced speakers, such as novelists and lecturers, have stage fright before taking the floor. ⁵In other words, it is perfectly normal to be nervous at the start of a speech. ⁶Your body is responding as it normally would to any stressful situation—by producing more adrenaline. ⁷This sudden shot of adrenaline is what makes your heart race, your hands shake, your knees knock, and your skin perspire.

____ 3. ¹If you walk down just about any city street in America, you will encounter countless billboards, posters, bumper stickers, and bus and cab displays, each with a separate advertising appeal. ²Your kitchen cupboard is probably full of product packages and labels, each containing at least one sales message. ³Go to the racetrack and you will see two-hundred-mile-an-hour race cars carrying advertising worth $75 million per year. ⁴Go to a tennis tournament, a jazz festival, or a golf match, and you will find corporate sponsors, such as the makers of cigarettes, sodas, or blue jeans. ⁵Go to a movie and you will find that marketers have paid a handsome sum to have your favorite stars use their products in the film. ⁶Almost anywhere you go, you will encounter advertisements of all types and sizes reminding you to buy an endless stream of products.

(Continues on next page)

___ 4. [1]In almost every society in the world, couples have become engaged in some way before marrying. [2]Engagement serves a variety of functions for the couple. [3]It provides a clear indication that marriage is about to occur. [4]Due to the exclusive nature of the relationship, personal and interpersonal testing can continue with less threat from competitive forces. [5]A more thorough awareness of shared and nonshared values, marital-role expectations, and future aspirations can be examined. [6]Engagement provides the final opportunity prior to the legal union for each person to understand himself or herself in relation to the other. [7]It is likely that many couples view an engagement as a kind of trial marriage, including sexual intimacy, the sharing of certain financial obligations, and, in some instances, living together.

___ 5. [1]The pattern of life for most Europeans between 1600 and 1800 centered on the struggle to stay alive. [2]At least once a decade, climatic conditions—usually a long period of summer rainfall—would produce a devastatingly bad harvest, which in turn would result in widespread malnutrition, often leading to serious illness and death. [3]A family might survive for a time by eating less, but eventually, with its meager stocks exhausted and the cost of grain high, the human costs would mount. [4]The substitution of grass, nuts, and tree bark for grain on which the peasants depended almost entirely for nourishment was inadequate to sustain healthy life.

MAIN IDEAS: Test B

The following paragraphs have main ideas that may appear at various places within the paragraph. Identify the topic sentence of each paragraph by filling in the correct sentence number in the space provided.

____ 1. [1]Hunger and thirst represent two of the most potent drives in our day-to-day lives. [2]But psychologists have identified a number of secondary drives that are also extremely powerful forces. [3]One such secondary drive is the need for achievement. [4]Most of us are motivated by the satisfaction of striving for and attaining a level of excellence in our chosen endeavors. [5]Another powerful secondary drive is the need for affiliation. [6]Put simply, this is the widespread human need for friendship. [7]A third type of secondary drive is the need for power. [8]Some people are very much influenced by their need to have an impact on those around them.

____ 2. [1]When Chevrolet began to sell its Nova cars in Latin America, hardly anyone would buy them. [2]The company finally learned that Spanish speakers read the car's name as the Spanish phrase *no va*, meaning "doesn't go"! [3]Like Chevrolet, many American companies have learned the hard way that they need to know their customers' language. [4]When Pepsi-Cola ran its "Come Alive with Pepsi" ads in China, the consumers laughed. [5]The company had not translated its slogan accurately. [6]In Chinese, it came out as "Pepsi brings your ancestors back from the dead."

____ 3. [1]In the South, the Civil War destroyed half the region's farm equipment and killed one-third of its draft animals. [2]The death of slavery also ended the plantation system. [3]The number of farms doubled from 1860 to 1880, but the number of landowners remained the same. [4]The size of the average farm dropped by more than half, as sharecropping and tenancy rose. [5]A shortage of cash forced Southern farmers to borrow against future crops. [6]Crop liens and high credit costs kept a lot of black and white farmers trapped in a cycle of debit and poverty. [7]So at the very time the rest of the economy was consolidating after the Civil War, Southern agriculture was marching off in the opposite, less efficient direction.

(Continues on next page)

_____ 4. [1]First, the good news: Americans are definitely eating more healthful meals. [2]We are consuming greater amounts of such high-fiber foods as whole-grain breads, fruits and vegetables, which are believed to help prevent certain cancers and other diseases. [3]At the same time, we are substituting relatively low-fat foods for higher-fat ones—for example, eating fish instead of red meat, drinking skim milk instead of whole. [4]The bad news is that our snack foods are not nearly as healthful. [5]Between meals, we often revert to eating large amounts of fat. [6]For instance, sales of ice cream and potato chips are going through the roof. [7]Another drawback of the snack foods is that they have almost no fiber. [8]As eating-behavior experts have concluded, we try super-hard to eat healthfully at mealtimes—but then undo some of the good work by "rewarding" ourselves with snacks that are bad for us.

_____ 5. [1]What does it take to achieve extraordinary success? [2]Educational psychologist Benjamin Bloom did a study of high achievers and found that drive and determination, not great natural talent, led to their success. [3]The study included America's top performers in six fields: concert pianists, Olympic swimmers, sculptors, tennis players, mathematicians, and research neurologists. [4]Development of Bloom's subjects began when parents exposed the child to music, swimming, scientific ideas, and so forth, "just for fun." [5]At first many of the children were quite ordinary in their skills. [6]One Olympic swimmer, for instance, remembers repeatedly losing races as a ten-year-old. [7]At some point, however, the children began to get recognition for their abilities and pursued them more actively. [8]After more successes and encouragement, the youngsters began "living" for their talent. [9]Most spent many hours each day practicing their skills. [10]This continued for many years before they reached truly extraordinary heights of achievement.

MAIN IDEAS: Test C

A. The following paragraphs have main ideas that may appear at various places within the paragraph. Identify the topic sentence of each paragraph by filling in the correct sentence number in the space provided.

____ 1. [1]Unlike women in other ancient societies, Egyptian women were not entirely subordinated to men. [2]Although polygamy was permitted, it was not common; the basic social unit was the monogamous family. [3]Even the pharaoh, who could keep secondary wives and concubines, had a chief wife. [4]Women were not secluded. [5]They could own and inherit property and engage in business. [6]The Egyptians of the New Kingdom also permitted queens to act as royal regents, giving them the power to rule in the pharaoh's absence. [7]For instance, Queen Hatshepsut of the Eighteenth Dynasty "controlled the affairs of the land." [8]In monumental statues from the Eighteenth Dynasty, some queens were depicted on the same scale of size as their husbands, while statues of anyone else had to be much smaller.

____ 2. [1]Childhood experiences can influence how we feel about being touched. [2]Little girls, for example, are generally kissed and cuddled more than little boys. [3]As a consequence, women often are more comfortable with touching than men are. [4]Also, Latin Americans and southern Europeans, for instance, casually touch each other far more than northern Europeans and most Americans. [5]Furthermore, our willingness to touch and be touched is affected by the social circumstances. [6]Even men who are generally uneasy about touching may hug one another at an exciting sporting event. [7]Thus our feelings about physical contact with others are affected by our childhood experiences, cultural background, and social context.

____ 3. [1]Many bank robbers and home thieves are caught and convicted in this country. [2]However, the American criminal justice system is not as well equipped to deal with white-collar crime as it is to handle street crime. [3]Unlike a robbery, a stock or insurance fraud is complex and difficult to unravel. [4]Local law enforcement officials commonly lack the skills and resources necessary to tackle crimes outside the sphere of street crime. [5]Federal agencies will handle only the more serious white-collar crimes. [6]And the handful of white-collar criminals who are prosecuted and convicted are given a slap on the wrist. [7]Street criminals who steal $100 may find their way to prison, while the dishonest executive who embezzles $1 million may receive a suspended sentence and a relatively small fine. [8]Federal statistics indicate that embezzlers at banks steal nine times more than bank robbers. [9]Yet whereas 91 percent of bank robbers end up in jail, only 17 percent of the embezzlers go to jail.

____ 4. [1]Andy and Sharon live in a small house with their two children in rural farm country. [2]Andy farms and works part-time in the local grocery store, while Sharon works part-time as a cook in a diner. [3]Although they earn only about $20,000 a year, they're happy, have the things they want, and think of themselves as doing pretty well. [4]Leslie

(Continues on next page)

recently moved to the "big city" to attend a private college. ⁵Although her parents pay all her expenses and give her $750 a month for "extras," Leslie constantly complains about how difficult it is to be poor, and many of her affluent friends feel the same way. ⁶Keith, a struggling young actor, works part-time nights as a guard and supports himself on about $900 a month. ⁷It's a difficult task, but Keith is happy with his life and considers himself economically comfortable. ⁸By the government's economic measurement, all these people except Leslie would be considered poor. ⁹Yet it is Leslie who feels poor. ¹⁰To a great extent, whether or not people consider themselves poor depends upon their expectations and the economic conditions of those around them.

B. (5.) The author has stated the central point of the following textbook selection in one sentence. Find and underline that sentence. Then, in the space provided, write the number of the sentence that contains the central point.

Aggression

¹Aggression can be defined as physical or verbal behavior intended to hurt someone. ²Scientists have learned there are various inborn and physical factors that influence the likelihood that an animal or human will be aggressive.

³Because aggression is a complex behavior, no one spot in the brain controls it. ⁴But in both animals and humans, researchers have found neural systems that assist aggression. ⁵When they activate those areas in the brain, hostility increases; when they deactivate them, hostility decreases. ⁶Tame animals can thus be provoked into rage, and raging animals into submission.

⁷There are also genetic influences on aggression. ⁸It has long been known that animals of many species can be bred for aggressiveness. ⁹Sometimes this is done for practical purposes (the breeding of fighting cocks). ¹⁰Sometimes, breeding is done for research. ¹¹Finnish psychologist Kirsti Lagerspetz took normal albino mice and bred the most aggressive ones together and the least aggressive ones together. ¹²After repeating the procedure for twenty-six generations, she had one set of fierce mice and one set of placid mice. ¹³Aggressiveness similarly varies among primates and humans. ¹⁴Our temperament—how intense and reactive we are—is partly something we bring with us into the world, influenced by our sympathetic nervous system's reactivity. ¹⁵Identical twins, when asked separately, are more likely than fraternal twins to agree on whether they have "a violent temper."

¹⁶Level of alcohol intake also influences neural sensitivity to aggressive stimulation. ¹⁷Both laboratory experiments and police data indicate that when people are provoked, alcohol unleashes aggression. ¹⁸Violent people are more likely (1) to drink and (2) to become aggressive when intoxicated. ¹⁹In experiments, intoxicated people administer strong shocks or higher pain buttons. ²⁰In the real world, people who have been drinking commit about half of rapes and other violent crimes. ²¹In 65 percent of homicides, the murderer and/or the victim had been drinking.

²²Aggressiveness also correlates with the male sex hormone, testosterone. ²³Although hormonal influences appear much stronger in lower animals than in humans, drugs that diminish testosterone levels in violent human males will subdue their aggressive tendencies.

_____ is the number of the sentence that states the central point.

MAIN IDEAS: Test D

A. The following paragraphs have main ideas that may appear at various places within the paragraph. Identify the topic sentence of each paragraph by filling in the correct sentence number in the space provided.

___ 1. [1]Technology revolutionized agriculture as inventions dramatically increased productivity on the farms. [2]Eli Whitney's invention of the cotton gin in 1793 permitted an individual to clean three hundred pounds of cotton in a single day—three hundred times more than could be cleaned by hand. [3]After the mechanization of wheat farming, the hours required to farm one acre dropped from sixty-one to three, and the per-acre cost of production fell from $3.65 to $0.66. [4]Machines entered every phase of agriculture—by 1890 some 900 companies were manufacturing such items as hay loaders, cord binders, seeders, rotary plows, mowers, and combines.

___ 2. [1]Shame is a painful emotion resulting from a strong sense of guilt or unworthiness. [2]It exists in all cultures. [3]But in Western culture in general and the United States in particular, shame is self-oriented, while in a country like Japan, it is linked not to the self but to others. [4]In America, if a child fails an exam, the child might feel terrible and be ashamed. [5]A Japanese child, on the other hand, would be ashamed not because he or she failed but because the failure resulted in shame for the child's parents. [6]Shame shows up in a similar way in the workplace. [7]In Japan, if a company doesn't make a profit as a result of worker laziness, the worker will be ashamed. [8]It's very hard to think of any American worker feeling ashamed that General Motors didn't make a profit. [9]The Japanese corporation works because it is part of a social system in which the failure of the individual reflects upon the group. [10]One feels shame for letting down the group, not the self.

___ 3. [1]A growing sexual permissiveness in the early 1900s evoked a series of severe responses. [2]Purity forces crusaded against indecent styles of dancing, immodest dress, and impure books and films. [3]One religious journal denounced popular dance styles as "impure, polluting, corrupting, debasing, destroying spirituality, [and] increasing carnality." [4]A bill was introduced in the Utah state legislature to fine and imprison women who wore, on the streets, skirts "higher than three inches above the ankle." [5]In the Ohio legislature it was proposed that cleavage be limited to two inches and that the sale of any "garment which unduly displays or accentuates the lines of the female figure" be prohibited. [6]Four states and many cities established censorship boards to review films, and many other cities broke up red-light districts and required licenses for dance halls.

___ 4. [1]The palaces of the civilization of Minoan Crete (at its peak from about 2000 to 1500 B.C.E.) lacked fortification, and the art lacked angry warlords. [2]Women's clothing, at least for the upper class, was so elegant that it would be eye-catching at a modern Milanese fashion show. [3]Two circumstances help to account for what was so obviously a world of peace and prosperity in Minoan Crete. [4]One was that, living on an island in

(Continues on next page)

an age unfamiliar with seaborne invasions, the Minoans must have felt insulated from foreign attack. ⁵The other was that a friendly climate and terrain suitable for pasturing and growing orchard crops (grapes, olives, nuts) freed the Minoans from heavy reliance on labor-intensive agriculture. ⁶This meant that not only did people have more leisure than their counterparts in agricultural societies, but produce was more diverse, providing a greater hedge against famine and allowing for long-distance trade in goods that were less easily produced elsewhere. ⁷To take but one example, the Minoans had plentiful wool and various kinds of natural dyes. ⁸Since wool, unlike linen, is easily dyed, Minoans were exporting "exotic" multipatterned luxury cloths to Egypt as early as about 2000 B.C.E.

B. (4.) The author has stated the central point of the following textbook selection in one sentence. Find and underline that sentence. Then, in the space provided, write the number of the sentence that contains the central point.

The Declining Birthrate in the United States

¹In 1800, the American birthrate was higher than the birthrate in any European nation. ²The typical American woman bore an average of seven children. ³She had her first child around the age of twenty-three and bore children at two-year intervals until her early forties. ⁴Had the American birthrate remained at this level, the nation's population would have reached 2 billion by 1990.

⁵Late in the eighteenth century, however, Americans began to have fewer children. ⁶Between 1800 and 1900, the birthrate fell 40 percent, most sharply among the middle and upper-middle class. ⁷Where the typical American mother bore seven children in 1800, the average number of children she bore had fallen to three and one-half in 1900. ⁸Instead of giving birth to her last child at the age of 40 or later, by 1900 the typical American woman bore her last child at the age of 33. ⁹The decline of the birthrate is such an important historical breakthrough that it has its own name: the demographic transition.

¹⁰What accounted for the declining birthrate? ¹¹In part, the reduction in fertility reflected the growing realization among parents that in an increasingly commercial and industrial society, children were no longer economic assets who would be productively employed in household industries or bound out as apprentices or servants. ¹²Instead, children required significant investment in the form of education to prepare them for respectable careers and marriages. ¹³The emergence of a self-conscious middle class concerned about social mobility and maintaining an acceptable standard of living also encouraged new limits on family size.

¹⁴The shrinking size of families also reflected a growing desire among women to assert control over their lives. ¹⁵Much of the impetus behind birth control came from women who were weary of an unending cycle of pregnancy, birth, nursing, and new pregnancy.

¹⁶Thus, an important decline in the American birthrate began in the late 1800s because of the new advantages to limiting family size and the growing desire among women to gain control over their reproductive lives.

_____ is the number of the sentence that states the central point.

SUPPORTING DETAILS: Test A

A. (1–6.) Complete the outline of the following textbook passage by adding the main idea and the missing major or minor details. Read the entire passage before beginning work on the outline. You may wish to number or check the major details within the passage as you read.

[1]There are a few major reasons for family violence. [2]One is stress, which is highest among the urban poor, families with a jobless husband, and those with four to six children. [3]Stress by itself, however, does not necessarily cause violence. [4]Another important factor is "a culturally recognized script" for violent behavior under stress in U.S. society (Straus et al., 1988). [5]The violence on television, corporal punishment in schools, and the death penalty, for example, convey the idea that violence is an acceptable solution to problems. [6]Research suggests yet one more reason for family violence: the tendency for marital violence is transmitted from one generation to another. [7]It has been found that most of the violent married individuals have, as children, seen their parents hit each other.

Main idea: _____

_____

1. _____

    a. _____

    b. Families with a jobless husband

    c. People with four to six children

2. U.S. "culturally recognized script" for violent behavior under stress

    a. _____

    b. Corporal punishment in schools

    c. _____

3. _____

(Continues on next page)

B. Answer the supporting-detail questions that follow the textbook passage.

[1]At the beginning of the eighteenth century, the United States lacked a strong educational system. [2]Apprenticeship in a trade was a major form of education, and formal schooling was largely limited to those who could afford to pay. [3]Even "free" schools often required the payment of tuition, and primary schools often required entering students to be literate already, barring students who had not been taught to read by their parents. [4]Many schools admitted students regardless of age, mixing young children with young adults in their twenties, and classrooms could contain as many as eighty pupils. [5]Few textbooks were available, and most learning amounted to monotonous repetition of facts. [6]School buildings were generally unpainted, over-crowded, and lacked blackboards or windows.

_____ 7. In general, the major supporting details of this paragraph are
   A. details of American life at the beginning of the eighteenth century.
   B. weaknesses of the American educational system at the beginning of the eighteenth century.
   C. problems with eighteenth-century America's school buildings.
   D. problems within the American educational system in previous centuries.

_____ 8. The first sentence of the paragraph provides
   A. the main idea.
   B. major details.
   C. minor details.

_____ 9. Sentence 5 provides
   A. the main idea.
   B. major details.
   C. minor details.

_____10. The major details of the passage are
   A. stages in the educational system.
   B. elements of the educational system.
   C. results of the educational system.
   D. questions about the educational system.

SUPPORTING DETAILS: Test B

A. (1–5.) Complete the map of the following textbook passage by filling in the main idea and the missing major supporting details. Read the entire passage before beginning work on the map. You may wish to number or check the major details within the passage as you read.

[1]Pollster Louis Harris has divided suburbs into four distinct categories based on income level and rate of growth. [2]Higher-income suburbs are categorized as either affluent bedroom or affluent settled. [3]The affluent bedroom communities rank at the highest levels in terms of income, proportion of persons employed in professional and managerial occupations, and percentages of homeowners. [4]Affluent settled communities tend to be older, and perhaps even declining in population. [5]They are more likely to house business firms and do not serve mainly as a place of residence for commuters.

[6]Harris has recognized that certain suburban areas are composed of individuals and families with low or moderate incomes. [7]Low-income growing communities serve as the home of upwardly mobile blue-collar workers who have moved from central cities. [8]Low-income stagnant communities are among the oldest suburbs and are experiencing the full range of social problems characteristic of the central cities.

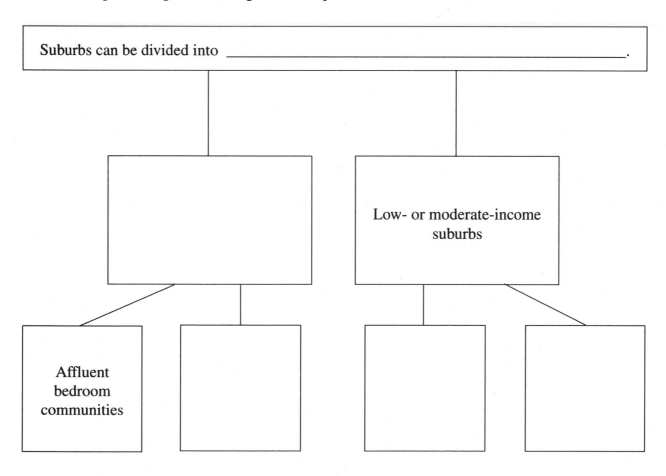

Suburbs can be divided into _____.

Low- or moderate-income suburbs

Affluent bedroom communities

(Continues on next page)

B. Answer the supporting-detail questions that follow the textbook passage.

   ¹Insomniacs may envy those who have no problem sleeping. ²However, too much sleep is also a sleep disorder. ³There are a couple of major causes of sleeping too much. ⁴One major cause of this problem is apnea, a condition associated with breathing difficulties during the night. ⁵In severe cases, the victim actually stops breathing after falling asleep. ⁶When the level of carbon dioxide in the blood rises to a certain point, apnea sufferers are spurred to a state of arousal just short of waking consciousness. ⁷Because this can happen hundreds of times in a night, apnea patients typically feel exhausted and fall asleep repeatedly the next day. ⁸Another cause of too much sleep is narcolepsy, a hereditary condition that causes victims to nod off without warning in the middle of a conversation or other alert activity. ⁹Narcoleptics will often experience a sudden loss of muscle tone upon expression of any sort of emotion. ¹⁰A joke, anger, sexual stimulation—all bring on a feeling of weakness. ¹¹Another symptom of the disorder is immediate entry into REM sleep, a state which produces frightening hallucinations that are in fact dreams that the narcoleptic experiences while still partly awake.

____ 6. In general, the major supporting details of the passage are
   A. types of insomniacs.
   B. causes of apnea.
   C. causes of getting too much sleep.
   D. symptoms of narcolepsy.

____ 7. Specifically, the major details are
   A. apnea and narcolepsy.
   B. insomnia and sleeping too much.
   C. exhaustion and repeated falling asleep during the day.
   D. a sudden loss of muscle tone, a feeling of weakness, immediate entry into REM sleep.

____ 8. Sentence 8 provides
   A. the topic sentence.
   B. a major detail.
   C. a minor detail.

____ 9. Sentence 11 provides
   A. the topic sentence.
   B. a major detail.
   C. a minor detail.

____10. According to the passage, apnea patients often fall asleep during the day
   A. when they experience any sort of emotion.
   B. because they have not slept at all at night.
   C. because of exhaustion from poor quality sleep.
   D. after they experience REM sleep.

Name _____

Section _____ Date _____

SCORE: (Number correct) × 10 = _____ %

SUPPORTING DETAILS: Test C

A. Answer the supporting-detail questions that follow the textbook passage.

> ¹After a period of squabbling, domestic chickens sort themselves into a reasonably stable "pecking order." ²Thereafter, when competition for food occurs, all hens defer to the dominant bird, all but the dominant bird give way to the second, and so on. ³Conflict is minimized because each bird knows its place. ⁴This process is an example of dominance hierarchy, a social arrangement in which animals establish a rank for members of the social unit, thereby eventually reducing aggression. ⁵Dominance in male bighorn sheep is reflected in the size of their horns. ⁶The larger the horn, the higher in the hierarchy a male bighorn sheep will be. ⁷Wolf packs are organized so that each sex has a dominant or "alpha" individual to whom all others are subordinate.

____ 1. The main idea of the paragraph is expressed in sentence
    A. 1.
    B. 2.
    C. 4.
    D. 7.

____ 2. The major details of this paragraph are
    A. examples of the main idea.
    B. questions about the main idea.
    C. problems relating to the main idea.
    D. reasons for the main idea.

____ 3. The second major detail is introduced in sentence
    A. 1.
    B. 3.
    C. 5.
    D. 7.

4–5. Complete the following study notes that summarize the passage.

Dominance hierarchy _____

_____

Ex.— _____

_____

(Continues on next page)

B. (6–10.) Outline the following textbook passage. Read the entire passage before beginning work on the outline. You may wish to number or check the major details within the passage as you read.

¹All relationships, unless they remain at the casual, small-talk level, experience growth that usually goes through five specific levels. ²The first, called initiating, involves the participants assessing each other in various areas—such as their clothing, physical attractiveness, and beliefs and attitudes. ³From these observations, they begin to make judgments about each other. ⁴Experimenting, the second stage, involves making a conscious effort to seek out common interests and experiences. ⁵Participants express their ideas, attitudes, and values and observe how the other person reacts to them. ⁶At this stage of the relationship, everything is generally pleasant, relaxed, and uncritical. ⁷Many relationships stay at this particular stage—the participants enjoy the level of the relationship but show no desire to pursue it further. ⁸The third level is known as the intensifying stage. ⁹At this stage, participants have already decided that they like each other a lot. ¹⁰They tell each other private things about their families and friends. ¹¹And they begin to share their frustrations, imperfections, and prejudices. ¹²Participants begin to use nicknames for each other and develop a "shorthand" way of speaking. ¹³Trust becomes important. ¹⁴The fourth stage, integrating, is the point at which the participants' individual personalities begin to merge. ¹⁵People begin to expect to see them together. ¹⁶Each of them is able to predict and explain the behavior of the other. ¹⁷The final coming-together stage of a relationship is the bonding stage. ¹⁸In this stage the participants make some sort of formal commitment that announces their relationship to those around them.

Main idea: _____

_____

1. _____: Participants assess each other in areas such as looks, beliefs, and attitudes.

2. Experimenting: In an effort to seek out common interests and experiences, participants express their ideas, views, and values and are uncritical with each other.

3. _____: Participants know they like each other a lot, share private personal information, begin to use nicknames for each other; trust becomes important.

4. _____

_____

_____

5. _____

_____

SUPPORTING DETAILS: Test D

A. Answer the supporting-detail questions that follow the textbook passage.

[1]More and more companies are interested in international marketing of their products and services. [2]In developing a framework in which to conduct international business, managers have two general strategies to choose from. [3]A global strategy is a standardized, worldwide product and marketing strategy. [4]The firm sells the same product in essentially the same manner throughout the world. [5]In Ford's global strategy, it merges its United States, European, Asian, and Latin American operations into one huge organization. [6]The goal is to create cars in standardized categories to be sold worldwide. [7]Ford management hopes to reduce the company's costs dramatically by engineering products only once, rather than multiple times for different markets. [8]Under a multinational strategy, the firm treats each national market differently. [9]Products and marketing strategies are developed to appeal to the customs, tastes, and buying habits of specific national markets. [10]Software maker Microsoft pursues a multinational strategy by creating products for specific markets, such as software that can read Japanese characters. [11]Microsoft also staffs its overseas sales and distribution operations with local workers, who understand the culture and customer.

____ 1. The major details of the paragraph are types of
  A. companies.
  B. managers.
  C. general international strategies.
  D. buying habits of particular national markets.

____ 2. The main idea of the paragraph is best expressed in
  A. sentence 1.
  B. sentence 2.
  C. sentence 3.
  D. sentence 9.

____ 3. The second major detail of the paragraph is introduced in
  A. sentence 3.
  B. sentence 4.
  C. sentence 5.
  D. sentence 8.

____ 4. Ford is presented as an example of
  A. automotive marketing.
  B. a global strategy.
  C. reduction of costs.
  D. a multinational strategy.

(Continues on next page)

B. (5–10.) Complete the map of the following textbook passage by filling in the main idea and the missing supporting details. Read the entire passage before beginning work on the map. You may wish to number or check the major details within the passage as you read.

¹For more than thirty years, Lawrence Kohlberg studied the ways that young men arrived at moral judgments. ²On the basis of the thought processes shown for moral decisions, Kohlberg described three levels of moral reasoning. ³The first level is preconventional morality. ⁴People at this level, under external controls, obey rules to avoid punishment or harm to people or property; or they act in their own self-interest. ⁵This level is typical of children aged 4 to 10. ⁶Kohlberg's next level of morality is conventional role conformity. ⁷People at this level have internalized the standards of authority figures. ⁸They are concerned about being "good," pleasing and caring for others, and maintaining the social order. ⁹This level is typically reached after age 10; many people never move beyond it, even in adulthood. ¹⁰Kohlberg's last level is morality of autonomous moral principles. ¹¹At this stage, morality is fully internal. ¹²People now recognize conflicts between moral standards and make their own moral judgments on the basis of principles of right, fairness, and justice. ¹³People generally do not reach this level of moral reasoning until at least age 13, or more commonly in young adulthood, if ever.

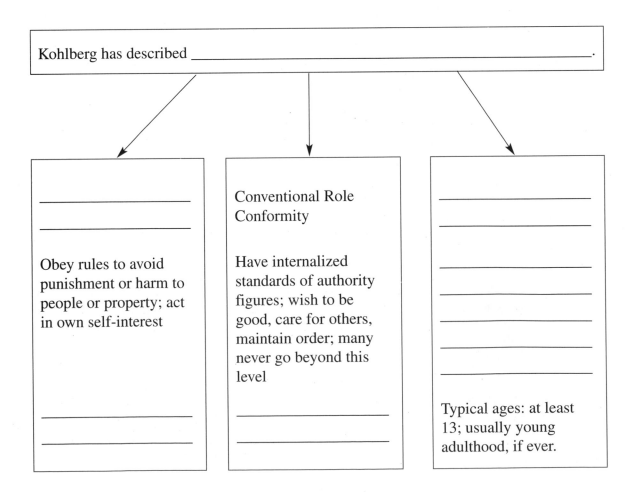

Kohlberg has described _____.

_____

_____

Obey rules to avoid punishment or harm to people or property; act in own self-interest

_____

_____

Conventional Role Conformity

Have internalized standards of authority figures; wish to be good, care for others, maintain order; many never go beyond this level

_____

_____

_____

_____

_____

_____

_____

_____

_____

Typical ages: at least 13; usually young adulthood, if ever.

IMPLIED MAIN IDEAS: Test A

In the space provided, write the letter of the sentence that best expresses the implied main idea of each of the following paragraphs.

____ 1. [1]In the early days of radio, one factor that kept FM radio from developing as much as AM was that more people had AM receivers than FM receivers. [2]Radios that could receive both AM and FM had not yet become popular, and it was not possible to pick up FM on a standard AM radio. [3]Moreover, many of the same people who owned AM stations owned FM stations; to simplify the programming effort, they would broadcast the same show over both frequencies. [4]Third, after World War II, the Federal Communications Commission (FCC) moved FM from the place it had originally occupied on the broadcast spectrum; this made all existing FM radios useless.

    A. Standard AM radios could not pick up FM.
    B. Several factors held back FM radio's development.
    C. Many owners of AM stations also owned FM stations.
    D. By moving FM to a different broadcast spectrum, the FCC made all existing FM radios useless.

____ 2. [1]Dolphins use a process called sonar to find their way and to find food. [2]They emit sound waves that bounce off objects and return, giving the dolphin information about distance, size, and density. [3]Some scientists think the dolphins can even "turn up" these sound waves and stun their prey. [4]They know that certain levels of sound waves could easily kill a large squid in a matter of minutes. [5]If these scientists are correct, dolphins could easily kill each other—yet they don't.

    A. Sea animals have wonderful skills at their disposal.
    B. Dolphins do not kill each other.
    C. Dolphin sonar is a powerful tool that appears to be used with skill and care.
    D. Sonar enables dolphins to find their way around by providing information on distance, size, and density.

____ 3. [1]Imagine a fundraiser comes to your door and asks for a five-hundred-dollar contribution. [2]You laughingly refuse, telling her that the amount is way out of your league. [3]She then asks for a ten-dollar contribution. If you are like most people, you'll probably be a lot more agreeable than if she hadn't asked for the huge contribution first. [4]Similarly, college students were stopped on the street and asked to agree to a substantial favor—acting as unpaid counselors for juvenile offenders two hours a week for two years. [5]Not surprisingly, no one agreed to such an outrageous request. [6]But when they were later asked the considerably smaller favor of taking a group of juvenile offenders on a two-hour trip to the zoo, half the people

(Continues on next page)

complied. [7]In comparison, only 17 percent of a control group of subjects who had not first received the larger request agreed.

   A. People are basically selfish and unwilling to help others.

   B. Only a small percentage of any group will agree to perform voluntary service.

   C. More people are willing to contribute money to a cause than donate their time.

   D. People are more willing to agree to a small favor after they have refused a large one.

____ 4. [1]In recent decades more young adults are returning to their parents' homes. [2]Most parents express satisfaction with the arrangement, especially when it is temporary and when the adult child is under age 22. [3]Parents appreciate help with household chores and with caring for younger children, and they enjoy sharing leisure activities. [4]Usually everyone is active and healthy. [5]But serious conflicts may arise, especially when a young adult is unemployed and financially dependent. [6]Disagreements may center on household responsibilities and the child's lifestyle: dress, sex, alcohol, drugs, and choice of friends. [7]The young adult is likely to feel isolated from peers and to have trouble establishing intimacy, while the parents may have to postpone renewing their own intimacy, exploring personal interests, and resolving marital issues. [8]The most difficult situation for parents seems to be the return of divorced or separated children with their own children.

   A. Adult children who return to their parents' home should provide help with household chores and with caring for younger children.

   B. A young adult who is unemployed and financially dependent makes life difficult for parents with whom he or she lives.

   C. People who live together in the same household are likely to have both positive and negative experiences.

   D. The return of adult children to their parents' homes can have both advantages and disadvantages.

IMPLIED MAIN IDEAS: Test B

In the space provided, write the letter of the sentence that best expresses the implied main idea of each of the following paragraphs.

___ 1. [1]South America contains the world's largest tropical rain forest—the Amazon. [2]It also contains a desert, the Atacama, that is one of the driest in the world. [3]It has steamy lowlands and icy high regions, including the Andes, mountains tall enough to have glaciers. [4]In just one South American country, Chile, we find a dry desert in the north and then, as we go southward, fertile green valleys, unspoiled pine forests, and then canyons carved by wild rivers. [5]In the southernmost part of Chile there are frigid mountains, and here, off the coast, there are frigid seas—this is the part of the world that is nearest to Antarctica. [6]Ecuador, a small country, nevertheless contains both tropical forests and snow-capped mountains.

   A. South America is a region of extreme geographic contrasts.
   B. Many people have an inaccurate idea of South America's geography.
   C. Of all South American countries, Chile and Ecuador are the most geographically diverse.
   D. South America is not a desirable vacation destination.

___ 2. [1]Intelligence is an ability to think logically and abstractly. [2]In contrast, wisdom is an ability to grasp paradoxes, reconcile contradictions, and make and accept compromises. [3]Because wise people weigh the effects of their acts on themselves and others, wisdom is particularly well suited to practical decision-making in a social context. [4]Whereas intelligence can figure out how to do something, wisdom asks whether it *should* be done. [5]Wise people, then, are better than others at solving social problems involving values—problems like easing racial tensions or deciding which divorcing spouse should have custody of the children.

   A. *Intelligence* is a word that describes our ability to think logically, allowing us to figure out how to do things.
   B. It is better to have wisdom than intelligence.
   C. Intelligence and wisdom are two different abilities, both important to human life.
   D. Humans have various natural abilities and skills that help them to understand and solve problems.

(Continues on next page)

___ 3. [1]In the United States and other Western nations, service-related industries have increased greatly, while manufacturing has declined over the last few decades. [2]Older manufacturing industries, which have traditionally paid fairly well, have been closed as overseas competition has increased. [3]In addition, jobs today require more education and skills. [4]The workplace is changing faster than ever, with new industries, such as biotech and computer-related industries, growing. [5]These industries require more technical skills. [6]Furthermore, there is more insecurity in the workplace. [7]Only 55 percent of all workers in a recent study believed that their companies provided job security, a decline from earlier studies. [8]Some of this insecurity is caused by the downsizing of firms. [9]In an attempt to become more competitive, companies have laid off workers, requiring the remaining workers to become more productive. [10]Finally, the growth of temporary workers, part-time workers, and contract workers has changed the vocational landscape. [11]Some predict that within a few years, half of all jobs will be held by these temporary workers.

   A. The workplace of today differs substantially from the workplace of several decades ago.

   B. Based on current trends, the workplace of the twenty-first century will be largely composed of temporary workers.

   C. The last several decades have seen enormous changes in lifestyle throughout the world.

   D. Biotech and computer-related companies are growing and changing the nature of the workplace.

___ 4. [1]Verbs are the most important of all tools. [2]They push the sentence forward and give it momentum. [3]Active verbs push hard; passive verbs tug fitfully. [4]Most verbs also carry somewhere in their imagery or in their sound a suggestion of what they mean: *flail, poke, dazzle, squash, beguile, pamper, swagger, wheedle, vex*. [5]I would bet that no other language has such a vast supply of verbs so bright with color. [6]Don't choose one that is dull or merely serviceable. [7]Make active verbs activate your sentences. [8]Also, try to avoid verbs that end in a preposition; that preposition weakens the force of the verbs. [9]For example, don't "set up" a business that you can "establish." [10]Don't "come upon" an object that you can "discover," or "take hold of" one that you can "grab."

   A. There are two types of verbs: active and passive.

   B. Since verbs are the most important parts of sentences, writers should use active verbs, preferring colorful ones without prepositions.

   C. In addition to having meanings, verbs sometimes have sounds that suggest what they mean.

   D. A verb that ends in a preposition lacks the punch of a verb that carries all of the meaning itself.

IMPLIED MAIN IDEAS: Test C

A. In the space provided, write the letter of the sentence that best expresses the implied main idea of each of the following paragraphs.

____ 1. [1]In the summer of 1988, a forest fire destroyed over one-fourth of Yellowstone National Park. [2]Park officials had let the fire burn for several weeks before they took measures to put it out.

[3]The let-burn policy is based on the idea that naturally occurring forest fires contribute to the overall long-term stability of the forest environment. [4]Small forest fires destroy fallen trees and leaves on the forest floor before large amounts of this debris can accumulate and cause larger and more destructive fires. [5]The earlier practice of suppressing all fires may have contributed to the intensity of the 1988 Yellowstone fires because large amounts of tinder had built up on the forest floor. [6]Forest fires also maintain the diversity of plant and animal life. [7]Small fires destroy some tall trees and thus allow for the growth of low bushes and grasses that attract small animal wildlife.

[8]However, many people criticized the let-burn policy after the Yellowstone fire. [9]Local ranchers were concerned that elk and bison would be driven out of the park and compete with cattle herds for food. [10]Others questioned the safety of allowing a fire during a drought. [11]Many people were confused by a change in policy after a hundred years of anti-fire publicity. [12]Some ecologists pointed out the difficulty of determining what is "natural" in a forest that has been sustained by human activity.

[13]In the meantime, Yellowstone officials have announced a return to the no-burn policy that existed before 1970, at least until experts agree that letting forest fires burn themselves out is justified.

A. The Yellowstone fire of 1988 resulted in a controversy about whether the let-burn policy had more advantages or disadvantages.

B. The original no-burn policy for handling forests should never have been changed.

C. The suppression of fire in forests leads to a buildup of possibly dangerous tinder on the forest floor.

D. Managing natural resources should best be left in the hands of national park officials.

____ 2. [1]The eighteenth century saw the introduction of two crops from the New World, maize (Indian corn) and the potato. [2]Since maize can be grown only in areas with a great deal of sunny and dry weather, its cultivation spread through Italy and the southeastern part of Europe. [3]Whereas an average ear of grain would yield only about four seeds for every one planted, an ear of maize would yield about seventy or eighty. [4]That made it a "miracle" crop, filling granaries where they had been almost empty before. [5]The potato was an equally miraculous innovation for the European North. [6]Its advantages were numerous: potatoes could be grown on the poorest, sandiest, or wettest of lands where nothing else could be raised; they could be fitted into the smallest of patches. [7]Raising potatoes even in small patches was profitable because the yield of potatoes was extraordinarily abundant. [8]Finally, the potato provided an inexpensive means of improving the human diet. [9]It is rich in calories and contains many vitamins and minerals.

(Continues on next page)

A. Both Indian corn and the potato originated in the New World.
B. Two New World crops—maize and the potato—have both advantages and disadvantages.
C. Two New World crops became important innovations in Europe, one in the sunny, dry south and the other in the north.
D. The discovery of the New World led to various new benefits for Europeans.

B. (3–4.) Write out the implied main idea of each of the following passages.

[1]An aquatic algae (seaweed) called *algin* is used often in salad dressings, ice cream, and other food products to keep the ingredients from separating. [2]Algae have also made an appearance in the beauty industry. [3]For example, a trendy treatment called thallassotherapy is a modern version of a treatment that was first used in France at the turn of the century. [4]In thallassotherapy, the body is smeared with a seaweed wrap that is the consistency of creamed spinach. [5]The desired result is to make the surface of the skin appear moist. [6]Algae are also used in a variety of cosmetics, including creams and astringents. [7]Extracts from some brown algae have antibacterial properties. [8]Manufacturers of creams and lotions containing these extracts advertise the antiseptic nature of their products. [9]Moreover, several types of seaweed have become popular staples at health-food stores for use in soups, stews, and salads.

Implied main idea: _____

_____

The Writing Process

[1]Some writers compose entirely in their heads, feeling no need to go through several drafts before approving what they have written. [2]The celebrated philosopher Bertrand Russell stated that after thinking intensely for an entire year about a series of lectures he had agreed to give, he called in a secretary and proceeded "to dictate the whole book without a moment's hesitation." [3]Similarly, the American poet Wallace Stevens composed many of his finest poems during his daily walk to his office, revising only for punctuation and spelling after he had dictated them to his secretary. [4]William Faulkner confessed that he put off writing as long as he could (owing to laziness, he admitted), but once he began, he found it fun, writing "so fast that somebody said my handwriting looks like a caterpillar that crawled through an inkwell and out onto a piece of paper."

[5]More often, however, writers struggle to get their ideas down on paper. [6]Impatient with the notion that writing is spontaneous joy, Wolcott Gibbs once observed that the only man he "ever knew who claimed that composition caused him no pain was a very bad writer, and he is now employed in a filling station." [7]S. J. Perelman confessed at the end of his career that unlike technicians "who are supposed to become more proficient with practice," he found "the effort of writing . . . more arduous all the time." [8]And the desire to escape from the labor of writing prompted the British novelist Anthony Trollope to advise all writers to attach a piece of cobbler's wax to the seat of their chairs to keep themselves securely fastened.

Implied main idea: _____

_____

IMPLIED MAIN IDEAS: Test D

A. In the space provided, write the letter of the sentence that best expresses the implied main idea of each of the following passages.

____ 1. ¹Antarctica represents one of the last resource frontiers left on the planet Earth. ²It is 98 percent covered by ice, and its low annual precipitation of less than 8 centimeters makes it a virtual desert. ³Its snow and ice hold 90 percent of the world's fresh water. ⁴The ice-covered land is inhospitable to life, but the edge of the ice and the surrounding offshore areas have a rich fauna—whales, penguins, seals, seabirds, fish, and an economically important shrimplike species known as krill. ⁵In the early 1900s, several nations claimed territory in Antarctica. ⁶Scientific interest in the region grew, and research activities evolved into cooperative research agreements among twelve nations (the United States, the Soviet Union, the United Kingdom, Belgium, Japan, South Africa, New Zealand, France, Australia, Norway, Chile, and Argentina), who were joined by four others (Poland, the Federal Republic of Germany, Brazil, and India) in signing the Antarctic Treaty that took effect in 1961. ⁷Sixteen more nations subsequently joined in the treaty. ⁸The treaty established Antarctica as a demilitarized, nonnuclear area and guarantees freedom of scientific investigation. ⁹The treaty also provides for free exchange of information among all researchers, and the participating nations agree not to assert any territorial claims while the treaty is in effect.

    A. Antarctica is a fascinating frontier with most of the world's fresh water and a rich variety of fauna.

    B. Antarctica has proven that the nations of the world can work together in peace.

    C. The Antarctic Treaty was originally agreed to by twelve nations who were then joined by four other nations.

    D. Since the early 1900s, scientific interest in resource-rich Antarctica led to cooperation among numerous nations.

____ 2. ¹In a merger, two or more firms combine to form one company. ²A vertical merger occurs between firms at different levels in a channel of distribution. ³The primary reasons for a vertical merger are (1) to assure adequate raw materials and supplies for products or (2) to increase available distribution outlets for them. ⁴In a backward vertical merger, a firm joins with a supplier; in a forward vertical merger, a producer buys a firm that distributes its products. ⁵For instance, several Hollywood movie studios have acquired video rental companies in order to profit from that lucrative distribution outlet. ⁶A horizontal merger joins firms in the same industry that wish to diversify and offer a more complete product line. ⁷For example, two banks might combine to offer expanded services to a larger customer base. ⁸A conglomerate merger combines unrelated firms. ⁹The most common reasons for a conglomerate merger are to diversify, to spur sales growth, or to spend a cash surplus that might otherwise make the holder a tempting target for a takeover effort. ¹⁰Conglomerate mergers may involve firms in totally unrelated industries. ¹¹Consider Metromedia International Group Inc., a venture that combines moviemaker Orion Pictures, several eastern European telecommunications companies, and Actava Group, the maker of Snapper lawn mowers.

    A. There are various reasons for firms of all types to merge.

    B. Mergers can be divided into three types, each with its own benefits.

    C. Hollywood movie studios that have acquired video rental companies illustrate the backward vertical merger.

    D. Companies must consider all the advantages and disadvantages of a merger before making a final decision to merge.

(Continues on next page)

B. (3.) Write out the implied main idea of the following paragraph.

   [1]Envy is a desire to acquire something that another person possesses. [2]People are envious when they wish they could have a house or car that a friend owns, a promotion that a coworker received, the kind of close relationships enjoyed by other couples, or anything else that they currently lack in their lives. [3]Typically, this occurs in situations in which people we like or associate with have things or take actions that threaten our definition of ourselves. [4]Someone who defines himself or herself as successful might become envious if a coworker was given a larger raise, a close friend purchased a more expensive car, or a friend received a higher grade point average. [5]On the other hand, jealousy is a fear of losing something to which we have become attached. [6]We are jealous when we fear losing a dating partner or spouse to another person or when we feel excluded from the company of someone we like or love.

   Implied main idea: _____

   _____

C. Read the following textbook passage and, in the space provided, write the letter of the sentence that best expresses the implied main idea.

_____ 4. [1]In preindustrial families, . . . a good index of neglect and indifference is found in journals kept by local doctors. [2]All of these doctors complained about parents leaving their infants and young children alone and untended for much of the day. [3]Rashes and sores from unchanged swaddling clothes afflicted nearly all infants.

   [4]Repeated accounts tell of children burning to death because they were left too close to an open hearth, and reports of unattended infants being eaten by barnyard pigs are frequent. [5]In the part of France where silkworms were raised, a peasant proverb acknowledged that children were neglected during the busy season: "When the silkworms rise, the kids go to paradise." [6]Indeed, throughout Europe, rural infants were most likely to die during the harvest season, when they were most neglected.

   [7]Even when parents were around their infants, they ignored them. [8]Mothers rarely sang or talked to their infants when they tended them, nor did they play games with them as the children grew older. [9]In fact, mothers didn't even refer to children by name, calling a child "it" or, in France, "the creature." . . .

   [10]Because of the high rates of infant mortality, it might be understandable that parents were somewhat reluctant to form intense emotional bonds with their babies. [11]But in some parts of France, parents typically did not attend funerals for children younger than 5, and there is widespread evidence that infant deaths often caused little if any regret or sorrow. [12]Instead, parents often expressed relief at the deaths of children, and many proverbs reflected this attitude. [13]Moreover, dead and even dying infants were often simply discarded like refuse and were frequently noticed "lying in the gutters or rotting on the dung-heaps."

   [14]Large numbers of legitimate infants whose parents were still living were abandoned outside churches or foundling homes. [15]Some scholars suggest that as many as half of the children abandoned in parts of France during the eighteenth century were abandoned by intact families.

   A. In preindustrial times, journals kept by doctors indicate that children were usually ignored.
   B. In preindustrial families, indifference toward children and neglectful childcare were common.
   C. Parents in preindustrial times expected their children to die at an early age.
   D. Child abuse has a long and ugly history.

RELATIONSHIPS I: Test A

A. Fill in each blank with an appropriate transition from the box. Use each transition once. Then, on the answer line, write the letter of the transition you have chosen.

A. also	B. first of all	C. other
D. third	E. until	

____ 1. [1]In Colonial America, washing clothing was so difficult that some households did it only four times a year. [2]The washing machine of the time was a "pounding barrel" containing a pole topped by a block of wood drilled with holes. [3]Moving the pole up and down caused water to suction through the clothes. [4]_____ the clothesline became common in the 1800s, wet clothes were spread on the ground or draped over a bush to dry.

____ 2. [1]Off-price stores are those stores that sell name-brand merchandise at prices below those in department stores. [2]They are able to do so for a couple of reasons. [3]_____, they take advantage of other people's mistakes and buy overstocked merchandise, irregulars, end-of-season items, and production overruns. [4]Second, they obtain merchandise at cut rates directly from manufacturers.

____ 3. [1]To get an image of an internal organ, a doctor sends an endoscope into the body, either through one of its natural openings or through one made especially for the purpose. [2]An endoscope is a flexible tube containing two separate bundles of fibers, each serving a different purpose. [3]One carries light into the opening, to illuminate the area being examined; the _____ picks up light reflected off the tissues and carries it back to the physician's eye or to the camera.

____ 4. [1]Even a quarrel can be done well or poorly. [2]According to some psychologists, there are several things to avoid when arguing. [3]One thing to avoid is bringing up unrelated issues from other situations. [4]You should also avoid using your knowledge of a person to humiliate him or her. A [5]_____ thing to avoid is pretending to agree with the other person while harboring resentment.

____ 5. [1]For most Americans, work is more than merely a means to food, shelter, and physical warmth. [2]When people work, they contribute to society. [3]The fact that they receive pay for their work indicates that what they do is needed by other people, and that they are a necessary part of the social fabric. [4]Work is _____ a major social mechanism for providing people with personal and social identities. [5]Much of who individuals are, to themselves and others, is interwoven with how they earn their livelihood.

(Continues on next page)

B. (6–9.) Fill in each blank with an appropriate transition from the box. Use each transition once. Then answer the question that follows.

also	another	eventually
for one thing		

¹In the late 1800s, the lines between social classes tended to blur in the large cities, much to the discomfort of the wealthy who struggled to separate themselves from the hoi polloi in various ways. ²(6)_____, the rich moved to the suburbs and employed other methods of residential segregation to isolate themselves. ³(7)_____ tactic to protect their exclusive status was to allow their children only to marry within their narrow group of acquaintances. They ⁴(8)_____ used sports and athletic clubs to set themselves apart. ⁵"Gentlemen and ladies," as they styled themselves, they wanted to compete only against opponents of similar dress, speech, education, and wealth. ⁶One way to exclude the masses in sports was to engage in those that only the very rich could play. ⁷Yachting and polo, for example, demanded nearly unlimited free time, expensive equipment, and a retinue of hired helpers. ⁸(9)_____, every major Eastern seaboard city had its exclusive yacht club.

_____10. The main pattern of organization of the above selection is
    A. list of items.
    B. time order.

RELATIONSHIPS I: Test B

A. Fill in each blank with an appropriate transition from the box. Use each transition once. Then answer the questions that follow.

another	finally	one

¹Cloning, the process of using genetic material to produce identical offspring, raises many difficult ethical questions which scientists have to answer. ²These questions stem from the various possible uses of cloning. ³(1)_____ such use may be to assemble genetically a child with superior traits—even if parents lack those characteristics. ⁴(2)_____ possible use of cloning technology could be to give parents the ability to set aside duplicates of their children, so that if one died, they could produce another child who looked exactly the same. ⁵Still another scenario predicts the possibility of using cloned embryos to produce a genetic duplicate if a child needed a bone marrow or kidney transplant, therefore eliminating any possible problem of immune rejection. ⁶(3)_____, cloning research may even make it possible someday for a woman to give birth to her own twin—a genetic copy of herself.

____ 4. The passage's main pattern of organization is
    A. list of items.
    B. series of events or stages.
    C. series of steps (directions).

____ 5. The total number of major details is
    A. two.
    B. three.
    C. four.

(Continues on next page)

B. (6–10.) Read the textbook passage below, and then answer the question and complete the map that follows. You may wish to number or check the major details within the passage before beginning to complete the map.

[1]Humanistic psychologist Carl Rogers believed that people are basically good and are endowed with tendencies to fulfill their potential. [2]Each of us is like an acorn, primed for growth and fulfillment, unless thwarted by an environment that inhibits growth. [3]Rogers theorized that a growth-promoting climate for people required three conditions. [4]The first of those conditions is genuineness. [5]According to Rogers, people nurture growth by being genuine—by dropping false faces and being open with their own feelings. [6]The second condition, said Rogers, is acceptance. [7]People also nurture growth, he said, by offering "unconditional positive regard"—an attitude of total acceptance toward another person. [8]We sometimes enjoy this gratifying experience in a good marriage, a close family, or an intimate friendship in which we no longer feel a need to explain ourselves and are free to be spontaneous without fear of losing another's esteem. [9]Finally, Rogers said that people nurture growth by being empathic —by nonjudgmentally reflecting feelings and meanings. [10]"Rarely do we listen with real understanding, true empathy," he said. [11]"Yet listening, of this very special kind, is one of the most potent forces for change that I know."

____ 6. The main pattern of organization of the above selection is
    A. list of items.
    B. time order.

7–10. Complete the map of the passage.

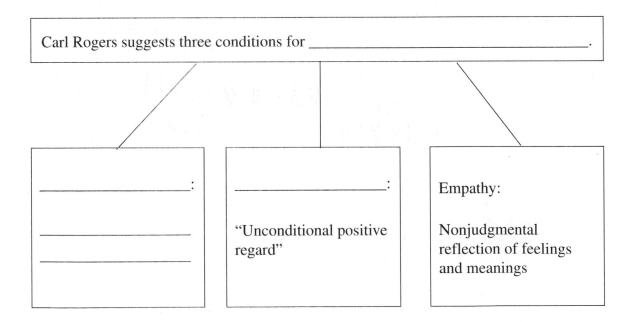

Carl Rogers suggests three conditions for _____.

_____:

_____

_____

_____:

"Unconditional positive regard"

Empathy:

Nonjudgmental reflection of feelings and meanings

RELATIONSHIPS I: Test C

Read each textbook passage and answer the questions or follow the directions provided.

¹The history of treatment for psychological problems gives sufficient reason for appreciating modern therapies. ²One of the more dramatic "cures" practiced by primitive "therapists" was a process called trepanning. ³A hole was bored, chipped, or bashed into the skull of the patient, presumably to relieve pressure or release evil spirits. ⁴Actually, trepanning may have simply been an excuse to kill people who were unusual, since many of the "patients" didn't survive the "treatment." ⁵During the Middle Ages, treatment for the mentally ill in Europe focused on demonology. ⁶Abnormal behavior was attributed to supernatural forces such as possession by the devil or the curses of witches or wizards. ⁷Exorcism, which often took the form of physical torture, was used to drive out the evil. ⁸The idea that the emotionally disturbed are "mentally ill" and that they should be treated compassionately emerged after 1793. ⁹This was the year Philippe Pinel changed the Bicetre Asylum in Paris from a squalid "madhouse" into a mental hospital by personally unchaining the inmates.

_____ 1. The author presents the supporting details in
   A. a list that could have been written in any order.
   B. the time order in which the details occurred.

_____ 2. The supporting details are
   A. modern therapies.
   B. ways of treating psychological problems.
   C. abnormal behaviors.
   D. supernatural beliefs during the Middle Ages.

3. A transition that introduces a major detail of the paragraph is _____.

¹Dr. Albert Merabian has researched interpersonal communications extensively, and he estimates that the majority of a message is composed of nonverbal communication. ²His studies show that 55 percent of the total message sent is composed of factors such as facial expressions, gestures, posture, and territoriality. ³Next most important is the tone used. ⁴The tone may indicate that you are being sarcastic, serious, romantic, and so forth. ⁵Tone is estimated to account for 38 percent of the total possible message. ⁶That leaves just 7 percent for the _____ component— the verbal part. ⁷The verbal message—the actual words—might be thought by many as the most important part of an message. ⁸In reality the words themselves are not nearly as important as the tone with which they are spoken and the nonverbal cues that accompany them. ⁹To focus on the words increases the chance of miscommunication.

_____ 4. The paragraph
   A. lists and discusses types of nonverbal communication.
   B. lists and discusses elements of a message.
   C. describes stages of communication.
   D. presents steps in good communication.

_____ 5. A transition that would fit the blank space is
   A. *third.*
   B. *fourth.*
   C. *later.*

(Continues on next page)

[1]Most social movements aim to change society, but they seek varying degrees of change. [2]Social movements can be classified into four types on the basis of their goals. [3]The first type is revolutionary movements, which seek total, radical change in society. [4]Their goal is to overthrow the existing form of government and replace it with a new one. [5]Revolutionary movements typically resort to violence or some other illegal action. [6]Examples include the revolution for independence in the United States, the Chinese Communist revolution, and the Castro-led revolution in Cuba. [7]The second type of social movement is reform movements. [8]They seek only a partial change in society. [9]They support the existing social system as a whole and want to preserve it, but they aim to improve it by removing its blemishes, typically through legal methods. [10]Each reform movement usually focuses on just one issue. [11]The civil rights movement seeks to rid society of racial discrimination. [12]The women's movement seeks to eliminate gender inequality. [13]The ecology movement seeks to put a stop to environmental pollution.

[14]Third, resistance movements seek to preserve an existing system by resisting social change. [15]The Ku Klux Klan and the United States Nazi party, for example, try to stop racial integration. [16]In Muslim countries, the Islamic revolution seeks to protect the traditional Islamic ways of life against Western influences. [17]Finally, expressive movements seek to change the individual, not society. [18]Many are religious, aimed at converting individuals to a particular faith. [19]These movements enable their members to express their sense of guilt, their joy of redemption, and their devotion to their religion. [20]Examples include the Moonies, Hare Krishnas, and other sects.

____ 6. The main pattern of organization of the above selection is
    A. list of items.
    B. time order.

7–10. Complete the outline of the passage. You may wish to number or check the major details within the passage before beginning to complete the outline.

Main idea: _____

_____

1. Revolutionary movements

   a. Goal: Overthrow and replace government

   b. Methods: _____

   c. Example: American Revolution

2. Reform movements

   a. Goal: Improve society with a partial change, usually regarding one issue

   b. Methods: Typically legal

   c. Example: _____

3. Resistance movements

   a. Goal: Preserve existing system

   b. Methods: Resisting social change

   c. Example: Ku Klux Klan

4. _____

   a. Goal: Change individual, not society

   b. Methods: Often religious

   c. Example: The Moonies

RELATIONSHIPS I: Test D

Read each textbook passage and answer the questions or follow the directions provided.

[1]It was not until after World War II that most Southerners felt the impact of air conditioning. [2]As one historian on the subject commented, "The air conditioner came to the South in a series of waves, and only with the wave of the 1950s was the region truly engulfed." [3]Gradually air conditioning spread to department stores, banks, government buildings, hospitals, schools, and finally, homes and automobiles. [4]Home air conditioning soared _____ the introduction in 1951 of an inexpensive, efficient window unit. [5]By 1960, 18 percent of all Southern homes had either window units or central air conditioning. [6]That number topped 50 percent in 1970 and almost 75 percent by 1980. [7]"The South of the 1970s could claim air-conditioned shopping malls, domed stadiums, dugouts, greenhouses, grain elevators, chicken coops, aircraft hangers, crane cabs, off-shore oil rigs, cattle barns, steel mills, and drive-in movies and restaurants," wrote one historian.

____ 1. The main pattern of organization of the above selection is
   A. list of items.
   B. time order.

____ 2. A transition that would fit the blank space is
   A. *second.*
   B. *after.*
   C. *next.*

[1]Americans have long believed in the attainability of a just social and political order. [2]But at no time was the spirit of a just society stronger than during the 1820s, 1830s, and 1840s, when literally hundreds of utopian communities were created. [3]Shaker communities were one of the earliest utopian "experiments." [4]Aspiring to live like the early Christians, Shakers adopted communal ownership of property and a way of life emphasizing simplicity. [5]Dress was kept simple and uniform; architecture and furniture were devoid of ornament. [6]Robert Owen's experimental community at New Harmony presented a striking contrast to the Shaker colonies. [7]Owen sought to establish common ownership of property and abolish religion. [8]At New Harmony the marriage ceremony was reduced to a single sentence, and children were raised outside of their natural parents' homes. [9]Another utopian experiment was perhaps the most notorious and successful—John Humphrey Noyes's Oneida Community. [10]Noyes established perfectionist communities that practiced communal owner-ship of property and "complex marriage." [11]Complex marriage meant that every member of the community was married to every member of the opposite sex. [12]The community also conducted experiments in eugenics—the selective control of mating in order to improve the hereditary qualities of children.

____ 3. The pattern of organization for the above selection is
   A. list of items.
   B. time order.

(Continues on next page)

4. A transition that introduces one of the major details of the paragraph is

_____.

____ 5. The total number of major details is
   A. two.
   B. three.
   C. four.

[1]Famous poets and writers have claimed for centuries that love stems from powerful emotions. [2]However, research has shown that feelings of love are at least in part influenced by various chemicals in the brain. [3]One group of chemicals that is just beginning to be understood is the pheromones—substances that promote sexual attraction in the opposite sex. [4]Experiments show that males release a chemical in their sweat that has been shown to be highly appealing to women—particularly during ovulation. [5]Similarly, women produce their own pheromones that draw men's interest—one actually can raise the level of testosterone in a man's bloodstream.

[6]In addition to pheromones, another chemical, phenylethylamine (PEA), plays a crucial role in helping people fall "in love." [7]Related closely to the addictive stimulant drugs called amphetamines, PEA actually causes people to feel a high from their relationship. [8]The "heart-throbbing" sensations new lovers describe and the feelings of excitement and infatuation that are part of new relationships are directly attributed to this chemical. [9]As with many addictive drugs, eventually the body builds up a tolerance to PEA and the strong feelings begin to wear off, usually within two years. [10]This explains why infatuation cannot last forever.

[11]A third group of chemicals—endorphins—appears to be at work in long-term relationships. [12]Endorphins are the body's natural pain relievers. [13]In addition, they produce a sense of security, tranquility, and calm. [14]During physical intimacy, endorphins are released into the bloodstream, creating the feeling of satisfaction and security common to long-term successful relationships.

____ 6. The main pattern of organization for the above selection is
   A. list of items.
   B. time order.

7. One transition that introduces a major detail of the selection is _____.

8–10. Complete the outline of the paragraph.

Main idea : _____

_____

1. _____

_____

2. Phenylethylamine (PEA)—Causes the high of new love, which wears off as the body builds up tolerance

3. _____—Are released into the bloodstream, creating a feeling of satisfaction, security, and calm

RELATIONSHIPS II: Test A

A. Fill in each blank with an appropriate transition from the box. Use each transition once. Then, on the answer line, write the letter of the transition you have chosen.

A. as a result	B. because of	C. even though
D. for instance	E. however	F. similarly

____ 1. [1]Only boxing rivaled baseball in popularity during the late 1800s. [2]Boxing began as a largely unstructured sport, but by 1900, businesspeople had reorganized the sport into a profitable activity. [3]_____ boxing remained illegal in most parts of America, it produced some of the first national sports heroes.

____ 2. [1]Sociologists have discovered that people seem to change their patterns of speech as social contexts change. [2]_____, a woman asking her son to mow the lawn might give a direct order ("Get that lawn mowed!") but use an indirect phrasing when addressing her husband ("The lawn's getting awfully high").

____ 3. [1]Can't get your ketchup out of the bottle? [2]Here's a great way to get ketchup flowing easily. [3]Simply insert an ordinary straw through the bottle's opening, pushing it straight down to the bottom. [4]_____, air is forced through the ketchup, giving it the environment it needs to pour easily—rather than "avalanche" out.

____ 4. [1]The increasing influence of the mass media contributes to the success of fast-food restaurants. [2]Without saturation advertising and the influence of television and other mass media, fast-food restaurants would not have succeeded as well as they have. [3]_____, the extensive advertising employed by such systems as H & R Block, Jenny Craig, and Pearle Vision Centers has helped make them resounding successes.

____ 5. [1]The "witch hunts" conducted by Joe McCarthy that began in the late 1940s were narrow-minded searches for Communist sympathizers in the United States. [2]These "witch hunts" took a heavy toll on the American movie industry. [3]One effect was that the studios fired more than three hundred actors, writers, and directors suspected of Communist leanings. [4]Many more were "blacklisted," which meant they weren't given work by the studios. Also, [5]_____ the hysteria over Communism, studios avoided making politically liberal films for fear of being branded as Communist.

____ 6. [1]When first produced, laundry bleach has no odor and is at its highest potency level. [2]_____, being on the shelf for a length of time (five to eight days) causes the solution to begin to break down chemically. [3]As it breaks down, the chlorine in the mixture gives off a gas, which is the reason certain bleaches exhibit a strong smell.

(Continues on next page)

B. Label each item with the letter of its main pattern of organization.

<blockquote>

A Definition and example   c Contrast

B Comparison   D Cause and effect

</blockquote>

_____ 7. [1]The wealthy of ancient Egypt lived in splendid villas that opened onto fragrant gardens and shady groves. [2]Their meals included many kinds of meat, poultry, cakes, fruit, wine, and sweets. [3]They ate from vessels of alabaster, gold, and silver, and adorned themselves with costly jewels. [4]However, the life of the poor was wretched. [5]Laborers in towns lived in mud-brick hovels whose only furnishings were stools, boxes, and a few crude pottery jars. [6]A surviving verse from the Middle Kingdom tells of the "weaver in the workshop, with knees against his chest," who "cannot breathe air," and who is "beaten fifty strokes" if he does not keep up with his work.

_____ 8. [1]Projection is an unconscious process of seeing one's own shortcomings in others. [2]For example, a greedy shop owner may cheat many of his customers, yet consider himself a pillar of the community and a good Christian. [3]How does he justify to himself his greed and dishonesty? [4]He believes that everyone who enters his store is bent on cheating him any way he or she can. [5]In reality, few, if any, of his customers share his motives, but he projects his own greed and dishonesty onto them.

_____ 9. [1]The rapid growth of industry in the United States resulted in a series of events that led to the Great Depression. [2]Because of the success of industry, much of the country's wealth ended up in the hands of a few. [3]As a result, the average American did not have enough money to buy all the products that were being manufactured. [4]The lack of consumers caused companies to produce less. [5]Needing fewer workers, they let old employees go and were unable to hire new ones. [6]Workers therefore had less and less money, causing industry to collapse even more. [7]As industries shut their plants and workers lost their jobs, banks across the country failed. [8]In 1930, the first full year of the depression, 1,300 banks closed their doors. [9]During the next two years, another 3,700 closed.

_____ 10. [1]History never repeats itself exactly, but there are close parallels, such as that between the American Revolution and the Vietnam War. [2]In both cases, an extremely powerful country was fighting thousands of miles from home against a relatively small native army, which was supported and supplied by a third country. [3]In the case of the Revolution, France was the third country; in the case of Vietnam, it was the Soviet Union. [4]Just as the British, with their command of the sea, could land troops wherever they wished on the Atlantic coast, so could the United States, with its air superiority, airlift troops wherever it wished in Vietnam. [5]Both wars were extremely unpopular at home. [6]But the most striking of the resemblances between the two is that while both great powers often defeated their enemies in large battles, neither was eventually able to win the war.

RELATIONSHIPS II: Test B

Read each paragraph and answer the questions that follow.

A. ¹When a person's position in society is derived primarily through inheritance, we call this ascribed status; that is, a person's position in society is fixed (or ascribed to him or her by others) on the basis of family background or genetic inheritance. ²Racial, ethnic, and religious differences, as well as gender, often serve as the basis for ascribed status. ³The caste system in India has long been an extreme example of a social structure based on ascribed status. ⁴Each level in society is known as a caste. ⁵Everyone is born belonging to a specific caste. ⁶The caste of the parents thus generally determines the status of their children, regardless of ability or merit.

____ 1. The main pattern of organization of the selection is
   A. definition-example.
   B. cause-effect.
   C. comparison and/or contrast.

2. The transition that signals the pattern of organization is _____.

B. ¹One of the factors that greatly influenced the development of the West was a simple product: barbed wire. ²Cheap, easy to string for hundreds of miles, and able to contain aggressive range animals, barbed wire was the key to the success of the agricultural effort. ³Because of that simple product, the once unlimited range was reduced to private holdings by barbed wire fences, and agriculture on newly protected lands grew. ⁴Nomadic herds of wild animals were restricted and died out, and the cattle and sheep industries could no longer rely upon unobstructed access to public land for forage. ⁵These changes in turn led to social and transportation system changes which tamed the West.

____ 3. The main patterns of organization of the selection are list of items and
   A. definition-example.
   B. cause-effect.
   C. comparison and/or contrast.

4. One transition that signals the pattern of organization is _____.

C. ¹Capitalists say that market forces should determine both products and prices and that it is healthy for people to strive after profits. ²They believe the potential for profit encourages people to develop and produce new products desired by the public, while workers are motivated to work hard so that they can make as much money as possible in order to purchase most goods. ³In contrast, socialists believe that profit is immoral, that it represents *excess value* extracted from workers. ⁴Karl Marx made the point that because an item's value represents the work that goes into it, there can be no profit unless workers are paid less than the value of their labor. ⁵Profit, then, represents an amount withheld from workers. ⁶To protect workers from this exploitation, socialists believe that the government should own the means of production, using them not for

(Continues on next page)

profit, but to produce and distribute items according to people's needs rather than their ability to pay.

___ 5. The main patterns of organization of the selection are list of items and
    A. definition-example.
    B. cause-effect.
    C. comparison and/or contrast.

6. The transition that signals the pattern of organization is _____.

D. [1]There are three main sources of large-scale cultural change. [2]The first is an alteration in the natural environment. [3]A change in the climate, a shortage of wheat or gasoline or some other resource, a sudden rise or fall in population—all force people to adapt. [4]They cannot go on living exactly as they did in the past. [5]The second cause of cultural change is contact with groups whose norms, values, and technology are different. [6]Cultural contact may be friendly or hostile, voluntary or involuntary, mutual (trade relations or a student exchange program) or one-sided (an invasion by military forces or technical advisors who impose their way of doing things). [7]The third source of cultural change is *discovery* and *invention*. [8]*Discovery* is uncovering of new knowledge about, or new uses for, something that already exists (such as oil in Mexico, the structure of genes, or the subculture of adolescents). [9]*Invention* is a recombination of existing knowledge and materials to create something new (such as the steam engine, the airplane, the cubist style of painting, or democracy). [10]Any one of these sources can lead to major change in a group's overall design for living.

___ 7. The main patterns of organization of the selection are list of items and
    A. definition-example.
    B. cause-effect.
    C. comparison and/or contrast.

8. One transition that signals the pattern of organization is _____.

E. [1]When Charles Dickens told the story of the French Revolution in his classic novel *A Tale of Two Cities*, he based much of his tale on solid historical fact. [2]History books mention the wastefulness of nobility; in like manner, Dickens tells of a French nobleman who required four servants just to bring him a cup of hot chocolate. [3]History books detail the sorry conditions of the prisons; similarly, Dickens writes of dreadful diseases that overcame prisoners, who often died before their sentences could be carried out. [4]But the most memorable features of *A Tale of Two Cities* are the characters, who are Dickens's own creations and have little to do with history. [5]The villain Madame Defarge, for instance, never really existed. [6]And history does not mention the heroic Sydney Carton or his famous sacrifice.

___ 9. The main patterns of organization of the selection are list of items and
    A. definition-example.
    B. cause-effect.
    C. comparison and/or contrast.

10. One transition that signals the pattern of organization is _____.

RELATIONSHIPS II: Test C

A. Read the textbook paragraph below. Then answer the question and complete the outline that follows.

> ¹In many companies, an invisible barrier still keeps women from reaching the executive suite. ²What are the reasons for this barrier? ³Researchers have found that most women tend not to be in the "pipeline" that leads to the top—marketing, sales, and production—positions related to the corporate bottom line. ⁴Instead, women are more likely to be working in human resources or public relations. ⁵Some say the reason women aren't in the "pipeline" positions is the male corporate culture. ⁶Men, who dominate the executive suite, tend to stereotype potential leaders as people who look like themselves. ⁷They also stereotype women as better at providing "support." ⁸Another fundamental reason for the barrier to women's entering the executive suite is that most women—even those who are in pipeline positions—lack mentors, successful executives who will take an interest in them and teach them the ropes.

____ 1. The main organizational patterns of the paragraph are list of items and
   A. definition-example.
   B. cause-effect.
   C. comparison.
   D. contrast.

2–5. Complete the outline of the paragraph by writing in the heading and the missing supporting details.

Main idea: _____

_____

1. _____

_____

   a. Men tend to stereotype potential leaders as those who look like themselves.

   b. _____

_____

2. _____

_____

(Continues on next page)

B. Read the textbook passage below. Then answer the question and complete the map that follows.

[1]Mutualism is a relationship in which two organisms live together or cooperate with each other for mutual benefit. [2]For example, termites eat wood but are unable to digest its cellulose. [3]The cellulose is digested by protozoa that live in the termite's gut. [4]Termites benefit from the presence of the protozoa by getting food digested, and the protozoa benefit by being protected by the termite's body. [5]In fact, under normal conditions the protozoa would be unable to live outside of the termite's body.

[6]Another interesting example of a mutualistic relationship is that of ants and acacia trees in Central and South America. [7]For a long time, scientists knew that the bull thorn acacia housed large numbers of ants. [8]Careful study of this relationship has revealed the reason. [9]The acacia tree provides a home for ants in the form of large thorns on its stem. [10]Sometimes ten or fifteen ants can fit into one thorn. [11]The tree also produces special growths on its leaves called beltian bodies. [12]Chemical analysis of these structures revealed that they are full of glycogen, which is also called animal starch. [13]The plant has a biochemical pathway that produces food used by ants. [14]The acacia derives benefits too. [15]Ants, protective of their food and housing, attack any predators that attempt to eat the acacia. [16]In addition, the ants destroy other plants that, if allowed to grow, would shade the acacia and cut off its light. [17]Bull thorn acacias are often found standing alone in open clearings because the ants have mowed down all the surrounding vegetation.

_____ 6. The passage's main pattern of organization is
  A. definition-example.
  B. cause-effect.
  C. comparison and/or contrast.

7–10. Complete the map of the passage by writing in the main idea and the missing supporting details.

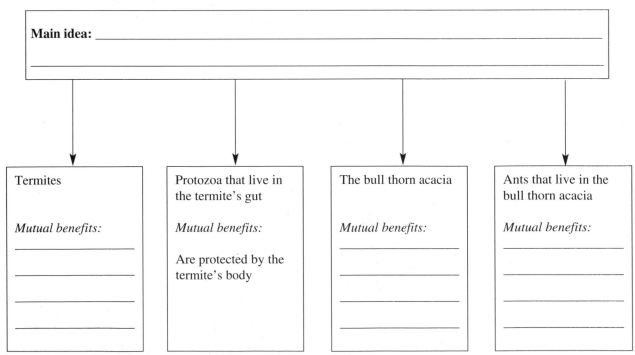

| **Main idea:** _____ |
| _____ |

Termites	Protozoa that live in the termite's gut	The bull thorn acacia	Ants that live in the bull thorn acacia
Mutual benefits: _____ _____ _____ _____	*Mutual benefits:* Are protected by the termite's body	*Mutual benefits:* _____ _____ _____ _____	*Mutual benefits:* _____ _____ _____ _____

RELATIONSHIPS II: Test D

A. Read the textbook passage below. Then answer the question and complete the outline that follows.

[1]The population of Europe as a whole, estimated roughly at 205 million by 1800, had risen to 274 million by 1850, and to 320 million by 1870. [2]Various reasons for the rapid population growth in Europe have been suggested. [3]Several explanations support the notion of improved health. [4]One contributing factor to this continued growth may have been a decline in the virulence of certain fatal diseases as a result of the cyclical potency of microbes. [5]Certainly the curbing of cholera, through the adoption of sanitary reforms, and smallpox, as Edward Jenner's technique of vaccination gained gradual acceptance after 1796, help to explain the population trend. [6]Also, the availability of less expensive foods of high nutritional value—most notably the potato—and the ability to transport foodstuffs cheaply by rail meant European populations would not suffer as much from undernourishment as in the past. [7]The population increase was probably also the result of rising birth rates caused by earlier marriages. [8]As serfdom declined, peasants tended to set up households at a younger age. [9]The spread of cottage industries provided an alternate income source, allowing more rural couples to marry and set up households even without the inheritance of land.

_____ 1. The organizational patterns of the passage are list of items and
    A. definition-example.
    B. comparison and/or contrast.
    C. cause-effect.

2–5. Complete the outline of the paragraph by writing in the main idea and the three missing supporting details.

Main idea: _____

_____

1. Less fatal illness
    a. Decline in certain fatal diseases due to cyclical potency of microbes
    b. _____
    c. Curbing of smallpox due to vaccination

2. _____
    a. Availability of less expensive foods of high nutritional value (especially the potato)
    b. Ability to transport food cheaply by rail

3. _____
    a. As serfdom declined, peasants tended to set up households at younger age
    b. Cottage industries allowed more rural couples to set up households even if they inherited no land to work

(Continues on next page)

B. Read the textbook paragraph below. Then answer the question and complete the map that follows.

¹Whether a nation has a presidential or a parliamentary system makes a big difference in the identity and powers of the chief executive. ²First of all, people become president by winning elections, and sometimes winning is easier if you can show the voters that you are not part of "the mess in Washington." ³For instance, neither Bill Clinton nor George W. Bush held national office before becoming president; and Barack Obama insisted, during his campaign, that his relative lack of Washington experience was an asset. ⁴Prime ministers are selected from among people already in Parliament, and so they are always insiders. ⁵They may or may not have any real personal following at the time they are appointed. ⁶Gordon Brown was not well known in Britain outside his own Labour Party before he became prime minister in 2007.

⁷Presidents and prime ministers also differ in how they choose cabinet members. ⁸Presidents choose cabinet members from outside Congress. ⁹Under the Constitution no sitting member of Congress can hold office in the executive branch. ¹⁰In contrast, the persons chosen by a prime minister to be in the cabinet are almost always members of Parliament. ¹¹This is one way by which the prime minister exercises control over the legislature. ¹²If you were an ambitious member of Parliament, then you would not be likely to antagonize the person who appointed people to important posts.

¹³Finally, presidents have no guaranteed majority in the legislature. ¹⁴A president's party often does not have a congressional majority. ¹⁵In contrast, a prime minister's party (or coalition) always has a majority in Parliament; if it did not, somebody else would be prime minister.

___ 6. The organizational patterns of the passage are list of items and
   A. definition-example.
   B. comparison and/or contrast.
   C. cause-effect.

7–10. Complete the map of the paragraph by completing the main idea and filling in the missing major supporting details.

```
┌──────────────────────────────────────────────────────────────────────┐
│ _____ between presidents and prime        │
│                                    ministers.                          │
└──────────────────────────────────────────────────────────────────────┘
        ╱                                              ╲
┌──────────────────────────┐          ┌──────────────────────────────┐
│        President          │          │       Prime Minister          │
│ Selected by national      │          │ _____     │
│ election, so doesn't      │          │                               │
│ have to be Washington     │          │ _____     │
│ insider                   │          │                               │
│                           │          │ Almost always chooses members │
│ _____   │          │ of Parliament as a way of     │
│                           │          │ exercising control over the   │
│ _____   │          │ legislature                   │
│                           │          │ Always has the majority (or   │
│ _____   │          │ would lose position as prime  │
│                           │          │ minister)                     │
│ _____   │          │                               │
└──────────────────────────┘          └──────────────────────────────┘
```

INFERENCES: Test A

A. Read each passage below. Then write the letter of the **one** statement after each passage which is most logically supported by the information given.

   [1]Where does that road go? [2]How does a television work? [3]What is that tool used for? [4]Answering these questions may have no obvious benefit for you. [5]Exploration and curiosity appear to be motives directed toward no more specific a goal than "finding out." [6]Even animals will learn a behavior just to be allowed to explore the environment. [7]Animals also seem to prefer complexity, presumably because more complex forms take longer to know and are therefore more interesting. [8]Placed in a maze that is painted black, a rat will explore it and learn its way around. [9]The next time, given a choice between a black maze and a blue one, it will choose the blue one. [10]Apparently the unfamiliarity of the unknown maze has more appeal.

____ 1. The passage implies that curiosity
   A. occurs only to gain a practical benefit.
   B. is what separates people from animals.
   C. can lead to exploration.

____ 2. The author implies that rats
   A. fear the challenge of a maze.
   B. are more curious than most other animals.
   C. can see color.

   [1]What is it about humor that makes us laugh? [2]The clue can be found in the fact that almost all jokes contain a contradiction between two realities, usually a conventional and an unconventional one. [3]These two realities represent conflicting definitions of the same situation. [4]To make people laugh, we first make them clearly aware of their taken-for-granted conventional definition of a situation and then surprise them by contradicting that definition with an unconventional one. [5]Look, for example, at the following joke from a study by one researcher:

   [6]My wife comes home and says, "Pack your bags. [7]I just won $20 million in the California lottery."
   [8]"Where are we going? Hawaii? Europe?" I ask jubilantly.
   [9]She says, "I don't know where you're going, Doug, as long as it's out of here."

[10]The first two sentences set up in our mind the conventional assumption that the married couple will share the joy of winning the lottery. [11]The punch line strikes down that assumption with the unexpected, unconventional reality that a presumably loving wife wants to be free from her husband.

____ 3. The humor in the joke comes from the
   A. wife's good luck.
   B. husband's misunderstanding.
   C. places the husband suggested they might travel to.

____ 4. Humor
   A. is never related to serious issues.
   B. involves hearing what we expect.
   C. involves surprise.

(Continues on next page)

B. (5–10.) Read the passage below, from *Long Walk to Freedom*, Nelson Mandela's autobiography. It's about events that took place in the Robben Island prison in South Africa, where Mandela spent eighteen of his twenty-seven years in prison. Then put a check (✓) next to the **six** statements which are most logically supported by the information given.

pap: mush   *warders:* guards

¹Through a plastic-wrapped note hidden in our food drums, we learned in July of 1966 that the men in the general section had embarked on a hunger strike to protest poor conditions. . . . ²Word was passed among us, and we resolved to initiate a sympathetic strike beginning with our next meal. ³A hunger strike consists of one thing: not eating.

⁴Because of the time lag in communications, the general prisoners probably did not learn of our participation for a day or so. ⁵But we knew that the news would hearten them. . . .

⁶During the first day of our strike, we were served our normal rations and refused to take them. ⁷On the second day, we noticed that our portions were larger and a few more vegetables accompanied our pap°. ⁸On the third day, juicy pieces of meat were served with supper. ⁹By the fourth day, the porridge was glistening with fat, and great hunks of meat and colorful vegetables were steaming on top. ¹⁰The food was positively mouthwatering. ¹¹The warders° smiled when we passed up the food. ¹²The temptation was great, but we resisted, even though we were being driven especially hard at the quarry. ¹³We heard that in the main section, prisoners were collapsing and being taken away in wheelbarrows.

¹⁴I was called to the Head Office for an interview with Colonel Wessels. . . . ¹⁵Wessels was a direct man and demanded to know why we were on a hunger strike. ¹⁶I explained that as political prisoners we saw protest to alter prison conditions as an extension of the anti-apartheid struggle. ¹⁷"But you don't even know why they are striking in F and G," he said. ¹⁸I said that did not matter, that the men in F and G were our brothers and that our struggle was indivisible. ¹⁹He snorted, and dismissed me.

²⁰The following day we learned of an extraordinary course of events: the warders had gone on their own food boycott, refusing to go to their own cafeteria. ²¹They were not striking in support of us, but had decided that if we could do such a thing, why couldn't they? ²²They were demanding better food and improved living conditions. ²³The combination of the two strikes was too much for the authorities. ²⁴They settled with the warders and then, a day or two later, we learned the authorities had gone to the general section and asked for three representatives to negotiate changes. ²⁵The general prisoners declared victory and called off the hunger strike. ²⁶We followed suit a day later.

_____ 1. Mandela and others were in a special section of the prison.

_____ 2. Prisoners in Mandela's section had to communicate secretly with those in the general section.

_____ 3. Before the hunger strike, inmate dinners in Mandela's section usually contained big pieces of vegetables and meat.

_____ 4. The prisoners in Mandela's section were served tempting food to bring back their strength after the fast.

_____ 5. The prisoners in Mandela's section were served tempting food to get them to stop their sympathetic hunger strike.

_____ 6. The prison officials recognized that the sympathetic strike in Mandela's section strengthened the strike in the general section.

_____ 7. It was easy to stay on the hunger strike.

_____ 8. Mandela and his fellow prisoners were highly motivated to show their support of their fellow prisoners.

_____ 9. The warders were more clever than the prisoners.

_____ 10. A hunger strike is one tool the weak can use to influence those in power.

INFERENCES: Test B

A. Following are the first three stanzas of William Blake's poem "The Fly." Read the poem, and then write the letter of the best answer to each question.

The Fly

Little Fly,
Thy summer's play
My thoughtless hand
Has brushed away.

Am not I
a fly like thee?
Or art thou not
A man like me?

For I dance,
and drink, and sing,
Till some blind hand
Shall brush my wing.

William Blake

____ 1. The speaker has
   A. played with the fly.
   B. lightly brushed the fly away.
   C. killed the fly.

____ 2. The speaker compares himself to
   A. summer's play.
   B. a fly.
   C. a dance.

____ 3. The speaker feels his life is
   A. not worth living.
   B. enjoyable.
   C. not enjoyable.

____ 4. We can conclude that the image of a wing being brushed symbolizes
   A. dancing.
   B. drinking.
   C. dying.

____ 5. The speaker feels death comes
   A. according to a plan.
   B. at random.

(Continues on next page)

B. (6–10.) Read the following textbook passage. Then put a check (✓) next to the **five** statements which are most logically supported by the information given.

[1]Without a native mythology, America had to manufacture its heroes. [2]Thus, when America turned one hundred years old, the American media created a suitably heroic model in the cowboys of the Wild West. [3]The image was of the steely-eyed cattle drivers living a life of reckless individualism, braving the elements, fighting off brutal Indian attacks; or of heroic lawmen dueling with sixguns in the streets at high noon. [4]This image became so powerful that it entered the American political mentality. [5]In fact, it shaped the images of Presidents Teddy Roosevelt, Lyndon Johnson, and Ronald Reagan. [6]However, the heyday of the cowboy lasted only about twenty years, from 1867 to 1887, and wasn't as glamorous or as romantically dangerous as it had been portrayed. [7]The modern politicians' comparison of drug-ravaged urban streets to the Wild West does a disservice to the West. [8]The famed cow and mining towns of Tombstone, Abilene, Dodge City, and Deadwood had fewer shootouts and killings in their combined history than modern Washington, D.C., has in a few months.

_____ 1. American mythology is influenced only by fact.

_____ 2. The author implies that most or all cultures need or want a native mythology.

_____ 3. The author feels that the Wild West of the 1800s was more dangerous than urban areas of today.

_____ 4. Images in a culture's media—regardless of how true they are—can influence the mentality of the people.

_____ 5. The author feels Presidents Teddy Roosevelt, Lyndon Johnson, and Ronald Reagan should not have been elected.

_____ 6. The author suggests that the positive qualities of the cowboy of the American media were incorporated into the public images of Presidents Roosevelt, Johnson, and Reagan.

_____ 7. The passage suggests that lawmen of the 1800s were not brave.

_____ 8. We can deduce that the cowboy got his name from his work with cattle.

_____ 9. The occupation of cowboy totally disappeared from America in the late 1880s.

_____ 10. Industries of the American West in the 1800s included mining and cattle ranching.

INFERENCES: Test C

A. Read the graph below. Then put a check (✓) by the **five** statements that are most logically based on the graph.

Unemployment, 1929–1942

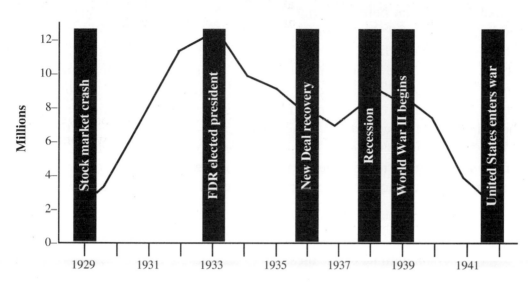

Source: *America and Its People*

_____ 1. In 1929, nobody was unemployed.

_____ 2. In the year after the stock-market crash, unemployment reached its highest point for the years 1929–1942.

_____ 3. It took about four years for unemployment to peak after the stock-market crash.

_____ 4. One problem FDR (Franklin Delano Roosevelt) faced after being elected president was great unemployment.

_____ 5. FDR had no success in lowering the unemployment rate.

_____ 6. The unemployment rate began to decrease after FDR became president.

_____ 7. By 1937, unemployment became as low as it had been before the stock-market crash.

_____ 8. The New Deal Recovery began to reverse in 1937.

_____ 9. Unemployment went up during World War II.

_____ 10. We can infer that during World War II, the unemployed found work in defense industries and the armed forces.

(Continues on next page)

B. (6–10.) Read the following passage from an essay on culture by American anthropologist Clyde Kluckhohn (1905–1960). Then put a check (✓) by the **five** statements which are most logically supported by the information given.

promiscuous: active sexually and relatively unselective about sexual partners
celibacy: going without sexual activity
reciprocities: exchanges

¹Every culture must deal with the sexual instinct. ²Some, however, seek to deny all sexual expression before marriage, whereas a Polynesian adolescent who was not promiscuous° would be distinctly abnormal. ³Some cultures enforce lifelong monogamy, while others, like our own, tolerate serial monogamy; in still other cultures, two or more women may be joined to one man or several men to a single woman. ⁴Homosexuality has been a permitted pattern in the Greco-Roman world, in parts of Islam, and in various primitive tribes. ⁵Large portions of the population of Tibet, and of Christendom at some places and periods, have practiced complete celibacy°. ⁶To us marriage is first and foremost an arrangement between two individuals. ⁷In many more societies marriage is merely one facet of a complicated set of reciprocities°, economic and otherwise, between two families or two clans.

_____ 1. In Polynesia, adolescent virginity is a virtue.

_____ 2. By "serial monogamy," the author means staying married to the same person until he or she dies.

_____ 3. By "serial monogamy," the author means staying married to one person at a time.

_____ 4. The sexual practices considered natural by a member of one society may be considered abnormal in another society.

_____ 5. Kluckhohn implies that marriage can be in part an economic decision.

_____ 6. Kluckhohn implies that homosexuality and celibacy are unnatural methods of expressing the sexual instinct.

_____ 7. The author suggests that all cultures should learn to express the sexual instinct in the same way.

_____ 8. The author suggests that a single human instinct may be expressed in a variety of ways.

_____ 9. The passage implies that the differences in sexual expression between societies are based on genetics.

_____ 10. The passage implies that the basis for the differences in sexual expression between societies is largely cultural.

INFERENCES: Test D

A. Read the following textbook passage. Then put a check (✓) by the **six** statements which are most logically supported by the information given.

¹Is eyewitness testimony, in fact, often inaccurate? ²Stories abound of innocent people who have wasted years in prison because of the testimony of eyewitnesses who were sincerely wrong. ³In the United States alone, some 80,000 trials a year hinge on eyewitness testimony. ⁴So even dozens of such cases would not prove that eyewitness accounts are unreliable. ⁵To assess the accuracy of eyewitness recollections, we need to learn their overall rates of "hits" and "misses." ⁶One way to gather such information is to stage crimes comparable to those in everyday life and then solicit eyewitness reports.

⁷This has now been done many times, sometimes with disconcerting results. ⁸For example, at California State University—Hayward, 141 students witnessed an "assault" on a professor. ⁹Seven weeks later, when asked to identify the assailant from a group of six photographs, 60 percent chose an innocent person. ¹⁰No wonder eyewitnesses to actual crimes sometimes disagree about what they saw.

¹¹Of course, some eyewitnesses are more confident than others—and it's the confident witnesses jurors find most believable. ¹²So it is disconcerting that unless conditions are very favorable, as when the culprit is very distinctive-looking, the certainty of witnesses bears only a modest relation to their accuracy. ¹³Intuitive confidence does correlate somewhat with accuracy, especially through people who make positive identifications. ¹⁴Yet some people—whether right or wrong—chronically express themselves more assertively. ¹⁵That explains why mistaken eyewitnesses are so often persuasive.

¹⁶This finding would surely come as a surprise to members of the 1972 United States Supreme Court. ¹⁷In a judgment that established the position of the U.S. judiciary system regarding eyewitness identifications, the Court, we now realize, goofed. ¹⁸It declared that among the factors to be considered in determining accuracy is "the level of certainty demonstrated by the witness."

¹⁹Errors sneak into our perceptions and our memories because our minds are not videotape machines. ²⁰Rather, we construct our memories based partly on what we perceived at the time and partly on our expectations, beliefs, and current knowledge.

_____ 1. Eyewitness testimony is useless.

_____ 2. More than just a few guilty people have probably gone free.

_____ 3. Eyewitnesses who are wrong are very likely to know that they are wrong.

_____ 4. Two sincere eyewitnesses may give contradictory evidence.

_____ 5. An eyewitness who is not confident may be more accurate than one who is.

_____ 6. Separating out truth from fiction in a trial must be relatively easy.

_____ 7. Jurors must sometimes make very difficult judgments.

_____ 8. The author feels that an ordinary-looking culprit is harder to identify.

_____ 9. Our memories are a mixture of correctly and incorrectly remembered events.

_____ 10. Memories we are quite sure about are very likely to be 100 percent true.

(Continues on next page)

B. The passage below from *The Writing Life*, by Annie Dillard, is about writing a book. After reading the passage, using the definitions as needed, write the letters of the inferences which are most logically supported by the details of the passage.

hie you: hurry   *cache:* a place where supplies are hidden

¹To find a honey tree, first catch a bee. ²Catch a bee when its legs are heavy with pollen; then it is ready for home. ³It is simple enough to catch a bee on a flower: hold a cup or glass above the bee, and when it flies up, cap the cup with a piece of cardboard. ⁴Carry the bee to a nearby open spot—best an elevated one—release it, and watch where it goes. ⁵Keep your eyes on it as long as you can see it, and hie you° to that last known place. ⁶Wait there until you see another bee; catch it, release it, and watch. ⁷Bee after bee will lead toward the honey tree, until you see the final bee enter the tree. ⁸Thoreau describes this process in his journals. ⁹So a book leads its writer.

¹⁰You may wonder how you start, how you catch the first one. ¹¹What do you use for bait?

¹²You have no choice. ¹³One bad winter in the Arctic, and not too long ago, an Algonquin woman and her baby were left alone after everyone else in their winter camp had starved. . . . ¹⁴The woman walked from the camp where everyone had died, and found at a lake a cache°. ¹⁵The cache contained one small fishhook. ¹⁶It was simple to rig a line but she had no bait, and no hope of bait. ¹⁷The baby cried. ¹⁸She took a knife and cut a strip from her own thigh. ¹⁹She fished with the worm of her own flesh and caught a jackfish; she fed the child and herself. ²⁰Of course she saved the fish gut for bait. ²¹She lived alone at the lake, on fish, until spring, when she walked out again and found people.

___ 7. In comparing writing a book to finding a honey tree (as described by Thoreau), Dillard implies that
    A. writing a book is like being in danger of getting stung.
    B. an author finds his or her way through a book one step at a time.
    C. to write a book, one must love nature.

___ 8. The comparison of writing a book to finding a honey tree suggests that writing a book, in the end, is
    A. a doubtful goal.
    B. an impossible goal.
    C. a desirable goal.

___ 9. In writing, "You may wonder how you start, how you catch the first one. What do you use for bait?" Dillard means
    A. Where does one get the very first idea with which to begin a book?
    B. What does one use for income while writing a book?
    C. How does one begin to write a book on fishing?

___10. With the anecdote about the Algonquin mother, Dillon implies that
    A. the Algonquin woman has great wisdom about writing.
    B. getting started with a book requires a painful digging within oneself.
    C. writing a book can be a life-or-death matter.

PURPOSE AND TONE: Test A

A. In the space provided, indicate whether the primary purpose of each sentence is to inform (**I**), to persuade (**P**), or to entertain (**E**).

_____ 1. Recent surveys reveal that the average daily television use per household is seven hours.

_____ 2. Our neighbor, the dentist, just got a new license plate for his car; it reads "DR-DKAY."

_____ 3. People convicted of drunk driving should automatically lose their licenses and get jail terms.

_____ 4. Angora sweaters are made from the long, silky hair of Angora goats or rabbits.

_____ 5. The old *Mary Tyler Moore Show,* featuring a cast of likable characters with real and endearing human qualities, should be honored as the best show in the history of television.

_____ 6. When the robot was buried, its owner wrote on its gravestone, "Rust in piece."

B. Each of the following passages illustrates one of the tones named in the box below. In each space provided, write the letter of the tone that applies to the passage. Two tone choices will be left over.

A. angry and impassioned	B. compassionate and caring	C. egotistical
D. apologetic and confused	E. critical but amused	F. objective

_____ 7. Barbie is an airhead. She is the material girl par excellence, the original mall rat. Introduced by Mattel at the Toy Fair in New York in 1959 as "The Barbie Doll: A Shapely Teenage Fashion Model," the long-limbed, 11½-inch-tall clotheshorse has no soul and barely a personality but has been the most successful doll in history. Like a handful of other famous women who need only a first name—Madonna, Jackie, Cher—Barbie has been at the vanguard of fashion for years. But unlike her human counterparts, she is a perpetually pubescent girl instead of a woman, and the only things on her mind are what she wears and the turning of Ken's vinyl head.

_____ 8. People think I have it so easy because my parents still support me. What they don't realize is that sure, I'd like to have a job. But nothing ever works out for me. I worked for a while at a restaurant, but they insisted on putting me on the breakfast shift. Face it, I'm a night owl, and getting up in time to

(Continues on next page)

work early in the day is just impossible for me. I want a job like my friend Alice, who wears nice suits and carries a briefcase to work. I've applied for a couple of jobs like hers, but the people who interview me say I'm not qualified. So what am I supposed to do? Until I'm offered a job that is worth my time, I'm not going to lower myself to accept something that's beneath me.

_____ 9. Mascara, eye shadow, and eyeliner may be part of every modern woman's makeup kit. But it was the ancient Egyptians who first thought of adorning the eyes with artificial cosmetics. Writings and pictures from more than 6,000 years ago demonstrate their interest in decorating the eyes. Ancient recipes survive for the Egyptians' favorite green eye shadows, created from powdered copper ore. Many Egyptian writings mention kohl, a black paste used to darken the lashes and eyebrows and to line the eyes. Fashionable Egyptian men and women also were the first to use eye glitter, made from the shells of beetles crushed to a fine powder.

_____ 10. Laws should be passed to limit the personal wealth of overly rich Americans. One percent of American families control more than 40 percent of the nation's wealth. Many of them play and prosper while everyday folks struggle to survive. More than three million Americans are homeless, and many poor children suffer from malnutrition. Middle-class families, too, are affected by America's unequal distribution of wealth, with many parents unable to afford to send their children to college. We must join the many ordinary, hard-working Americans all across the country that are speaking out in favor of a more just and appropriate system of distribution of wealth. After all, the spoiled rich don't deserve to be rich.

PURPOSE AND TONE: Test B

A. Eight quotations in the story below are preceded by a blank space. Identify the tone of each italicized quotation by writing in the letter of one of these tones. (Two tone choices will be left over.)

A. angry	B. annoyed	C. apologetic
D. confused	E. frightened	F. grateful
G. ironic	H. matter-of-fact	I. optimistic
J. pleading		

The line for course registration wound nearly around the college gymnasium. Barbara and Carol, sophomores at the college, had been waiting in line an hour. During that time they had introduced themselves and swapped information on the teachers they liked and the courses they planned to take.

_____ 1. *"I just don't understand why we have to wait in line so long,"* Barbara said, frowning at the long line ahead of them.

_____ 2. *"It shouldn't be too much longer. The line seems to be moving with more speed now,"* Carol said cheerfully. *"Besides, the wait has given us the chance to get to know each other."*

When Carol reached the registration table, she signed up for four courses, including Psychology 201. Then she stood to the side to wait for Barbara.

_____ 3. *"I'd also like to register for Psych 201,"* Barbara told the man at the registration table.

_____ 4. *"I'm very sorry,"* the man said sincerely. *"I hate to tell students that they won't be able to take a course, but that one has already been filled. I am sorry."*

_____ 5. *"What do you mean it's been filled?"* Barbara asked. *"This is the first day of registration. How can it be filled already? That really stinks! What do I pay college tuition for when I can't register for a course I really need this semester?"*

"I'm sorry, but the course is closed," the man insisted.

_____ 6. *"Oh, can't you put just one more student down?"* Barbara asked. *"Please. Just one more?"*

The man shook his head no.

"Can she take my place in the class?" Carol asked the man. "After all, I only just signed up for it a minute ago. And I can easily take it another semester."

_____ 7. *"Well, I . . . Let me see . . . It's a little irregular, but . . . Well, I don't know,"* he said.

(Continues on next page)

"I'm equally interested in other courses," Carol added. "I really don't mind signing up for something else."

"Well, all right," the man agreed.

_____ 8. *"Thanks, Carol. Thanks a lot,"* Barb said. "After all, I'd say an hour is a short time to wait—for a new friend."

B. In the space provided, indicate whether the primary purpose of each passage is to inform (**I**), to persuade (**P**), or to entertain (**E**).

_____ 9. ¹Contrary to popular opinion, fish can drown! ²Here's how: Fish must extract oxygen from the water in order to live, the same way that we must get oxygen from the air. ³Therefore, if fish are in an aquarium, ocean, lake, or any other body of water that is poor in oxygen content, they can die. ⁴Remember the definition of "drowning" is dying from suffocation in water because access to oxygen is limited or cut off. ⁵So, even though fish live in water, they can also die in it—if the water is oxygen-poor.

_____ 10. ¹In the eyes of some, legalizing narcotics is a tantalizing cure-all for America's drug problem. ²It's time, they say, to stop pouring enormous resources into the war on drugs. . . .

³True, the war on drugs is not being won. ⁴The courts are overflowing with cases waiting to be tried. ⁵Huge seizures of narcotics stop only a small fraction of the drugs coming into the country. ⁶Countless dragnets snare only the small-time pusher, not the drug kingpin. ⁷Clearly, as it is being waged now, the national fight against drug abuse is futile.

⁸The only thing more costly than continuing the current war on drugs would be the legalization of narcotics; such a measure would claim innumerable human lives. ⁹Government figures estimate that crimes involving drug use cost society more than $58 billion a year. ¹⁰Substance abuse is linked with 52 percent of rapes committed, 49 percent of murders, 62 percent of assaults, and 50 percent of traffic fatalities and incidents of spousal abuse. ¹¹The legalization of narcotics could only push those figures higher.

PURPOSE AND TONE: Test C

Read each of the selections below. Then carefully consider the questions that follow, and write the letters of the best responses.

A. ¹Violence, of course, is rampant in the media. ²But it is usually set in some kind of moral context. ³It's usually only the bad guys who commit violent acts against the innocent. ⁴When the good guys get violent, it's against those who deserve it. ⁵Dirty Harry blows away the scum; he doesn't walk up to a toddler and say, "Make my day."

⁶But in some rock songs, it's the "heroes" who commit the acts. ⁷The people we are programmed to identify with are the ones being violent, with women on the receiving end. ⁸In a society where rape and assaults on women are endemic, this is no small problem, with millions of young boys watching on their TV screens and listening on their iPods.

⁹I think something needs to be done. ¹⁰I'd like to see people in the industry respond to the problem. ¹¹I'd love to see some women rock stars speak out against violence against women. ¹²I would like to see disc jockeys refuse air play to records and videos that contain such violence. ¹³At the very least, I want to see the end of the silence. ¹⁴I want journalists and parents and critics and performing artists to keep this issue alive in the public forum.

_____ 1. The primary purpose of this paragraph is to
   A. inform readers about violence in the media in the United States today.
   B. persuade readers that rock lyrics that promote violence should be opposed.
   C. entertain readers with descriptions of dramatic media images.

_____ 2. The tone of this paragraph can be described as
   A. indignant and determined.
   B. superior and mocking.
   C. understanding and tolerant.
   D. hurt and revengeful.

B. ¹Geologists study rocks. ²Archaeologists study old civilizations. ³And atmospheric chemists—the newest breed of scientist—study old air, the kind trapped in bubbles found in glaciers left over from the last ice age or in the ice sheets of Greenland or Antarctica. ⁴By studying the history of our atmosphere, these scientists can tell what the air was like in prehistoric times and measure how human activity over two thousand years has changed it. ⁵First the ice is cut into cubes, and then the air is sucked out into a vacuum chamber where it is stored in tubes. ⁶Finally, the carbon dioxide level is analyzed by a laser beam. ⁷It is believed that rising levels of carbon dioxide foretell a rise in temperatures around the world. ⁸Thus these scientists may be able to predict dangerous changes in climate and possibly the next ice age.

_____ 3. The primary purpose of this paragraph is to
   A. inform.
   B. persuade.
   C. entertain.

(Continues on next page)

_____ 4. The author's tone is
   A. straightforward but disbelieving.
   B. excited and cheerful.
   C. solemn and sympathetic.
   D. straightforward and matter-of-fact.

C. [1]I have a relative who never throws anything away. [2]This woman (in the interests of protecting her privacy, I won't tell you who she is. [3]Just let me say that I've known her forever and she shares a bedroom with my father) has a stack of *Reader's Digest* magazines five feet high. [4]"Someday I'm going to take all the 'It Pays To Increase Your Word Power' quizzes," she says when I suggest it's time to say goodbye to issues from, oh, say, 1974 to 1987. [5]In her garage are roughly four million cardboard tubes from rolls of toilet paper and paper towels. [6]"They're so useful for children's art projects," she says, ignoring the fact that her children are all in their mid-twenties. [7]Her kitchen cupboards are jammed with little aluminum foil pans from chicken pot pies. [8]"I could make individual lemon-meringue pies for a special dessert," she says. [9]"You've been saying that for fifteen years," I say. [10]"Well, someday I'm going to," she answers. [11]"Just as soon as I've gotten through all those 'Word Power' quizzes."

_____ 5. The primary purpose of this paragraph is to
   A. inform.
   B. persuade.
   C. entertain.

_____ 6. The author's tone is
   A. serious and critical.
   B. sentimental and optimistic.
   C. informal and humorous.
   D. surprised but compassionate.

D. [1]Young men who have committed minor crimes are generally locked up in jail with older, more hardened lawbreakers. [2]There the younger men merely learn to be better criminals. [3]A far better idea is to send young offenders to "boot camp." [4]Such camps have been set up in scattered areas around the country, and more should be established. [5]In the boot camps, modeled after the ones Army recruits go through, young offenders serve their time as they become more disciplined, increase their self-confidence, and learn to work as part of a team. [6]Instead of sitting in jail cells all day, the men cooperate in work projects, undergo a tough physical training program, and see other men functioning as positive role models. [7]"Graduates" of prison boot camp are more likely to become productive citizens than men who have spent their sentences in jail.

_____ 7. The primary purpose of this paragraph is to
   A. inform.
   B. persuade.
   C. entertain.

_____ 8. The author's tone is
   A. direct and concerned.
   B. bitter and cynical.
   C. contemptuous and sarcastic.
   D. outspoken but ambivalent.

PURPOSE AND TONE: Test D

Read each of the paragraphs below. Then carefully consider the questions that follow, and write the letters of the best responses.

A. ¹There is something as inevitable as labor that takes over around Christmas. ²I feel impelled to the kitchen. ³I feel deep hungers for star-shaped cookies and tangerine ices and caramel cakes, things I never think of during the rest of the year. ⁴Even when I have vowed to keep it simple, I have found myself making the deadly Martha Washington Jetties my mother made every year on the cold back porch. ⁵You have to make them in the cold because the sinful cream, sugar, and pecan fondant balls are dipped by toothpick into chocolate and held up to set before being placed on the chilled wax-papered tray. ⁶The chocolate dip, of course, constantly turns hard and must be taken into the kitchen and heated. ⁷My mother made Jetties endlessly because her friends expected them. ⁸We professed to find them too rich but ate them until our teeth ached. ⁹I still have the cut-glass candy jar they spent their brief tenures in.

_____ 1. The purpose of this paragraph is to
    A. give readers tips on celebrating a holiday.
    B. persuade readers to make Martha Washington Jetties.
    C. entertain readers by sharing a sweet experience.

_____ 2. The tone of the paragraph can be described as
    A. matter-of-fact and solemn.
    B. ironic and self-mocking.
    C. uncertain and bewildered.
    D. nostalgic and affectionate.

B. ¹The differences between complaints and personal criticisms are simple. ²In a complaint, a wife states specifically what is upsetting her, and criticizes her husband's *action*, not her husband, saying how it made her feel: "When you forgot to pick up my clothes at the cleaner's, it made me feel like you don't care about me." ³It is an expression of basic emotional intelligence: assertive, not belligerent or passive. ⁴But in a personal criticism, she uses the specific grievance to launch a global attack on her husband: "You're always so selfish and uncaring. ⁵It just proves I can't trust you to do anything right." ⁶This kind of criticism leaves the person on the receiving end feeling ashamed, disliked, blamed, and defective—all of which are more likely to lead to a defensive response than to steps to improve things.

_____ 3. The primary purpose of this paragraph is to
    A. inform the reader of two ways to communicate a problem: complaints and personal criticisms.
    B. persuade readers that complaints are a better way of communicating a problem than personal criticism.
    C. entertain readers with the drama of a husband-wife conflict.

_____ 4. The tone of the paragraph can be described as
    A. critical but understanding.
    B. superior and detached.
    C. explanatory and caring.
    D. distressed but optimistic.

(Continues on next page)

C. [1]It's easy to see why a lot of people aren't as successful at losing weight as I'm going to be. [2]They go for some crazy scheme that doesn't work. [3]Not me. [4]I'm going to do it the old-fashioned way and simply cut down on everything. [5]After I've lost twenty pounds, I may write a book about it.

[6]Come to think of it, later today I may call my publisher and ask if there'd be any interest in a book about my weight loss. [7]*How I Lost 20 Pounds in 20 Days,* I may call it. [8]That would be a good title, give or take a few days.

[9]It might even be a good idea if I started a diary the same day I start losing weight. [10]Maybe I'll start the diary tomorrow, too; then I'll have the book done at the same time I'm twenty pounds lighter.

[11]Of course, I don't want to get too thin. [12]I don't want to look drawn. [13]Doctors advise against going up and down too fast, so I don't want to overdo it. [14]Maybe I'll have an occasional dish of ice cream. [15]It might be better if I didn't try to get too thin too soon. [16]If I lose weight gradually, it might be a good idea if I didn't start the book right away, either. [17]I wouldn't want to finish the book before I'm finished losing weight.

____ 5. The purpose of this paragraph is to
   A. inform readers about a personal decision.
   B. persuade readers of the importance of a healthy weight.
   C. entertain readers by poking fun at an all-too-human approach to dieting.

____ 6. The tone of the paragraph can be described as
   A. serious and caring.   C. warm and respectful.
   B. playful and self-mocking.   D. analytical and instructive.

D. [1]Words can be more powerful, and more treacherous, then we sometimes suspect; communication more difficult than we may think. [2]We are all serving life sentences of solitary confinement within our own bodies; like prisoners, we have, as it were, to tap in awkward code to our fellow men in their neighboring cells. [3]Further, when A and B converse, their dialogue involves not two characters, as they suppose, but six. [4]For there is A's real self—call it A_1; there is also A's picture of himself— A_2; there is also B's picture of A—A_3. [5]And there are three corresponding personalities of B. [6]With six characters involved even in a simple one-on-one conversation, no wonder we fall into muddles and misunderstandings.

[7]Perhaps then, there are five main reasons for trying to gain some mastery of language:

[8]We have no other way of understanding, informing, misinforming, or persuading one another.

[9]Even alone, we think mainly in words: if our language is muddy, so will our thinking be.

[10]By our handling of words we are often revealed and judged. [11]"Has he written anything?" said Napoleon of a candidate for an appointment. [12]"Let me see his *style*."

[13]Without a feeling for language, one remains half-blind and deaf to literature.

[14]Our mother tongue is bettered or worsened by the way each generation uses it. [15]Languages evolve like species.

____ 7. The primary purpose of this paragraph is to
   A. inform readers about how to communicate.
   B. persuade readers of the importance of language skills.
   C. entertain readers with interesting observations about people.

____ 8. The tone of this paragraph can be described as
   A. serious and analytical.   C. ambivalent but optimistic.
   B. critical and ironic.   D. joking and affectionate.

ARGUMENT: Test A

A. (1–4.) In each group, one statement is the point of an argument, and the other statements are support for that point. Write the letter of the point of each group.

___ *Group 1*

A. My boss expects me to work overtime on a moment's notice.
B. Driving to work now takes me an hour.
C. I think I ought to look for another job.
D. I've worked at the restaurant for over a year, and I still haven't gotten a raise.

___ *Group 2*

A. Couples are marrying later than ever before.
B. Legal abortion and birth control devices are available.
C. Dropping fertility rates can be explained by changes in American society.
D. Fewer couples are opting for large families.

___ *Group 3*

A. A good, zestful laugh has a positive effect on various systems of the body.
B. During a hearty laugh, your muscles release tension as they tighten up and relax again.
C. One psychological effect of laughing is a feeling of well-being—like a "runner's high."
D. When you laugh, heavy breathing creates a vigorous air exchange in your lungs and a healthy workout for your respiratory system.

___ *Group 4*

A. The ultraviolet rays of the sun can cause skin cancer, particularly in fair-skinned people.
B. Up to 90 percent of all wrinkles are caused by the sun.
C. While people are out in the sun getting a tan, their skin is losing much of its natural moisture, causing the skin to look dry.
D. A suntan may not be so healthy or good-looking in the long run.

(Continues on next page)

B. Each point is followed by three statements that provide relevant support and three that do not. In the spaces, write the letters of the **three** relevant statements of support.

Point: The county should require residents to recycle newspapers, cans, and bottles.
A. When the county had a "Clean Up Our Streets" day, everyone pitched in.
B. By selling the materials to be recycled, the county could gain much-needed funds.
C. County residents should be taught to buy products that are not wastefully packaged.
D. Recycling contributes to a stronger environment by making the best use of limited resources.
E. It wouldn't be difficult for the county to give every home a recycling bin to use.
F. Recycling will help solve the problem of limited space in landfills.

5–7. *Items that logically support the point:* _____ _____ _____

Point: Many insects and spiders are beneficial.
A. By eating insects, crickets and spiders help to maintain the balance of nature.
B. Most spiders are not harmful.
C. Ants improve the soil by breaking down organic materials.
D. In regions of the Amazon River that flood each year, ants avoid drowning by building their nests in trees.
E. It is unknown why female black widow spiders sometimes kill and eat their mates after sex.
F. Bees not only produce honey; they also help to pollinate various crops.

8–10. *Items that logically support the point:* _____ _____ _____

ARGUMENT: Test B

A. For each paragraph, write the letter of the sentence that does **not** support the point of the argument.

[1]Our prisons do an inadequate job of rehabilitating prisoners. [2]Our recidivism rate—the percent of those released from prison who are later arrested for other crimes—runs somewhere between 30 and 80 percent, depending on the study. [3]The crime rate among former prisoners is actually much higher, for the recidivism rate represents only those who are rearrested. [4]To top it all off, for one reason or another, many guilty people are never even sent to jail. [5]Part of the reason for recidivism is a penal system that produces contempt and hatred—attitudes hardly conducive to law-abiding behavior.

____ 1. Which sentence is **not** relevant support for the argument that our prisons do an inadequate job of rehabilitating prisoners?
   A. Sentence 2
   B. Sentence 3
   C. Sentence 4
   D. Sentence 5

[1]Trappers should not use the steel-jaw leghold trap, used to trap animals for their fur. [2]In snapping shut on an animal's leg, the trap tears muscle and shatters bone. [3]Commonly, animals caught in leghold traps die slowly and painfully—from exposure, starvation, or lack of water. [4]Those who manage to break free, by chewing off part of their leg, are likely to die from infection. [5]Those still trapped and alive when the trapper returns are strangled or clubbed to death. [6]In any case, with the warmth of modern fabrics, it's absolutely unnecessary to make any fur coats at all.

____ 2. Which sentence is **not** relevant support for the author's argument that the steel-jaw leghold trap should not be used to trap animals?
   A. Sentence 2
   B. Sentence 3
   C. Sentence 4
   D. Sentence 6

[1]We need better police protection on campus. [2]So far this year, a dozen dorm rooms have been broken into; in each instance, valuables were stolen. [3]Within the past two months, several students have been mugged when they returned to their cars in campus parking lots. [4]If there were more plentiful parking near the center of campus, students wouldn't have to park in the more isolated lots at the outskirts of campus. [5]While walking back to their dorms from evening classes, several other students have been raped. [6]When I walk across the campus at night, I usually fail to see a single police officer or security guard. [7]There may be plenty of security guards protecting the equipment inside the college's buildings, but people are more important than property.

(Continues on next page)

_____ 3. Which sentence is **not** relevant support for the author's conclusion that better police protection is needed on campus?

    A. Sentence 2

    B. Sentence 3

    C. Sentence 4

    D. Sentence 5

B. For each group, read the three items of support (the evidence). Then write the letter of the point that is adequately supported by that evidence.

Group 1

Support:

> • Cell phones allow businesspeople to do two jobs at once—go to an appointment and make a business phone call.
> • If a car occupant is going to be late for a business or family event because of traffic, he or she can call and change the time of the meeting.
> • Drivers with cell phones can report accidents the minute they happen.

_____ 4. Which of the following conclusions is best supported by the evidence above?

    A. Everyone who drives a car should have a cell phone.

    B. Cell phones can be an asset.

    C. A cell phone can distract a driver and cause an accident.

    D. All companies should be required to buy cell phones for their employees.

Group 2

Support:

> • According to the U. S. Census Bureau, college graduates earn, during their working lives, over a million dollars more than high-school graduates.
> • A college degree increases intellectual curiosity and the ability to think logically.
> • People with a college degree tend to have increased interest in and responsiveness to the arts.

_____ 5. Which of the following conclusions is best supported by the evidence above?

    A. People without a college degree do not appreciate the arts.

    B. College's benefits are mainly academic.

    C. A college degree can have valuable financial and intellectual benefits.

    D. Everyone in our society should go to college for four years.

ARGUMENT: Test C

A. Each of the two points below is followed by six items, three of which logically support the point and three of which do not. In the spaces provided, write the letters of the **three** items that logically support each point.

Point: A stoplight should be put in at the intersection of Broad and Walnut.

A. That intersection has one of the highest accident rates of all the intersections in town.

B. A police officer should be stationed there during the early morning and later afternoon, when traffic is heaviest.

C. At Broad and Walnut, a driver cannot see the road in all directions without starting to pull out into the intersection.

D. Our town seems to care more about park equipment than it does about the safety of its intersections.

E. Many children have to cross the intersection at Broad and Walnut in order to get to school, so the safety of that intersection is especially important.

F. We pay plenty of taxes in this township.

1–3. *Items that logically support the point:*   _____   _____   _____

Point: Laws requiring motorcycle riders to wear helmets are a good idea.

A. Of the many motorcyclists who have had accidents, those not wearing helmets sometimes end up brain-dead.

B. The government should not pass laws to protect people in every area of their lives; otherwise, we'd need numerous other types of laws as well—prohibiting drivers from buying even one drink, prohibiting people from eating too many saturated fats, and so on.

C. Motorcyclists should sign organ donor cards so that if they have an accident and become brain-dead, at least someone will benefit.

D. It's the taxpayers who pay when motorcyclists without adequate insurance refuse to wear helmets and end up with horrible head injuries.

E. Even motorcyclists who wear helmets are sometimes greatly injured.

F. There's a precedent for requiring people to protect themselves—many states require people to use seatbelts.

4–6. *Items that logically support the point:*   _____   _____   _____

B. Read the following three items of support (the evidence). Then write the letter of the point that is adequately supported by that evidence.

Support:

- Yoga improves a person's posture, resulting in more energy and greater lung capacity.
- Stretching and relaxing muscles through yoga postures releases tension and helps the body to align properly.
- Holding yoga postures helps increase strength and balance.

(Continues on next page)

_____ 7. Which of the following conclusions is best supported by the evidence above?
   A. Yoga is one of the most popular forms of exercise today.
   B. Practicing yoga benefits the body in several ways.
   C. Yoga is not as beneficial as working out with weights.
   D. There are a number of ways to practice yoga.

C. Read the paragraphs below, and then write the letter of the best answer to each question that follows.

[1]Much of the surgery performed in United States hospitals is unnecessary. [2]For one thing, there are more than twice as many surgeons per capita in the United States as in England—and twice as much surgery. [3]Yet there is no reason to believe that Americans need twice as much surgery as the British. [4]Perhaps it's the American surgeons' bank accounts that "need" all those extra operations. [5]Some experts contend that two-thirds of all hysterectomies performed in the United States are unnecessary, yet the operation is the second most common for women in the country, with 600,000 hysterectomies being performed every year. [6]Twenty years ago, only 6 percent of births in the United States were accomplished through Caesarean sections; today that figure is close to 33 percent. [7]Yet there is no evidence that women have more difficulty bearing children now than they did twenty years ago.

_____ 8. Which statement is **not** relevant support for the argument that much of the surgery done in U.S. hospitals is unnecessary?
   A. Sentence 3
   B. Sentence 4
   C. Sentence 5
   D. Sentence 6

[1]Poverty is one important cause of shoplifting, as suggested by the evidence that poor people are more likely than others to shoplift and that shoplifting becomes more common when unemployment is high. [2]Another economic reason for shoplifting is frugal customers, ones who can afford to buy the things they need but are driven to steal them by a desire to stretch their budget. [3]In addition to economic motivations for shoplifting, there are also social-psychological ones. [4]The most common psychological cause is the sense of excitement and fun that shoplifters experience. [5]Young shoplifters should be pointed toward other exciting, more wholesome activities, such as sports. [6]Another social-psychological cause is the desire for social acceptance; youngsters in particular when asked why they shoplift say, "Because my friends are doing it."

_____ 9. Which statement is the point of the argument?
   A. Poverty is an important cause of shoplifting.
   B. Young people have different motives for shoplifting than adults.
   C. Economic and social-psychological motives are behind shoplifting.
   D. Shoplifting is a big and complicated problem in our society.

_____ 10. Which statement is **not** relevant support for the point of the argument?
   A. Sentence 1
   B. Sentence 2
   C. Sentence 5
   D. Sentence 6

ARGUMENT: Test D

A. Each of the two points below is followed by six items, three of which logically support the point and three of which do not. In the spaces provided, write the letters of the **three** items that logically support each point.

Point: It is better for environmentalists to work with, not against, timber companies.

    A. One conservation group has purchased forests to keep them out of the hands of timber companies.

    B. By working with timber companies, environmentalists can encourage less-damaging harvesting methods, such as leaving some trees to hold soil in place and shelter songbirds.

    C. In previous years, the timber companies and conservationists have strongly opposed each other.

    D. Timber companies that work with conservationists agree to avoid building steep logging roads, which encourage erosion.

    E. Environmentalists are working to preserve such endangered ecological sites as sand dunes in Florida's panhandle and prairies in the Midwest.

    F. Conservation groups are helping companies to maintain forests with selective cutting, instead of cutting them all down, and thereby gaining the support of communities, which welcome the continuation of timber-related jobs.

    1–3. Items that logically support the point: _____ _____ _____

Point: Animal tests do not necessarily reveal whether a drug will be safe or effective for humans.

    A. Penicillin, one of the safest drugs for humans, kills guinea pigs and hamsters.

    B. Computers can analyze a drug's chemical structure.

    C. A survey of two hundred drugs that had tested safe and effective for animals showed that 80 percent of the drugs proved harmful or ineffective for humans.

    D. Currently, the law requires that all drugs be tested on animals.

    E. Before being marketed, all drugs are tested on human volunteers.

    F. After testing safe for rats, mice, and other animals, the drug thalidomide caused serious birth defects in humans.

    4–6. Items that logically support the point: _____ _____ _____

B. Read the following three items of support (the evidence). Then write the letter of the point that is adequately supported by that evidence.

Support:

> - Among the Tasmanians of the South Pacific, the most dangerous type of hunting—swimming out to remote rocks in the sea to stalk and club sea otters—was assigned to women.
> - Women formed the bodyguard of Dahomeyan kings because they were thought to be particularly fierce fighters.
> - In most prominent American families of the eighteenth and nineteenth centuries, girls' education centered on needlework, music, dancing, and languages.

(Continues on next page)

___ 7. Which of the following conclusions is best supported by the evidence above?
  A. There were very few men among the Tasmanian and the Dahomeyan tribes.
  B. The women in those tribes were slaves.
  C. Women's roles have varied greatly from society to society.
  D. Tasmanian and Dahomeyan women had unnatural societal roles.

C. Write the letter of the sentence in each paragraph that does **not** support the point of the argument.

[1]Age at marriage is an important predictor of a marriage's success. [2]Teenagers have high divorce rates for various reasons. [3]Early marriage may lock a couple into a relationship neither one is mature enough to handle, restricting both partners' potential for growth. [4]This in turn makes the young husband and wife less able to deal successfully with the challenges all marriages face. [5]Studies show that remarriage at any age is also a challenge leading to more frequent divorce. [6]Studies also show that people who wait until their late twenties or later to marry have the highest chances of success at marriage.

___ 8. Which sentence is **not** relevant support for the author's argument that age at marriage is an important predictor of a marriage's success?
  A. Sentence 2   C. Sentence 5
  B. Sentence 3   D. Sentence 6

[1]Kübler-Ross's five stages of dying should not be overemphasized. [2]The recognition of those five stages is very important to an understanding of the dying process. [3]However, though the emotions that Kübler-Ross describes are common, not everyone goes through all five stages, and people may go through the stages in different sequences. [4]A person may go back and forth between stages—anger and depression, for example—or may feel both at once. [5]Instead of the orderly progression in Kübler-Ross's theoretical model, dying people may show "a jumble of conflicting or alternating reactions running the gamut from denial to acceptance, with a tremendous variation affected by age, sex, race, ethnic group, social setting, and personality" (Butler & Lewis). [6]Unfortunately, some health professionals feel that they have failed if they cannot bring a patient to "the ultimate goal, the big number *five*—'acceptance' of death" (Leviton).

___ 9. Which sentence is **not** relevant support for the argument that Kübler-Ross's five stages of dying should not be overemphasized?
  A. Sentence 2   C. Sentence 5
  B. Sentence 4   D. Sentence 6

[1]Genetic testing should be very limited. [2]Genetic information may be disseminated in a way that violates privacy. [3]Although medical data are supposed to be confidential, it is almost impossible to keep such information private. [4]A study at the University of Minnesota found that at least fifty people had access to each patient's medical charts. [5]Secondly, a genetic profile may be used to deny a job, insurance, or other benefits. [6]In fact, discrimination on the basis of genetic information has already occurred. [7]An informal survey found fifty cases in which people had been denied jobs, insurance claims, and other benefits because of their genes. [8]In addition, it might be extremely anxiety-producing for a person to learn that she or he has the gene for an incurable disease. [9]What is the point of knowing you have a potentially debilitating condition when you cannot do anything about it, especially if the financial costs of testing are very high? [10]At the same time, determining a person's genetic makeup may lead to early detection or prevention of a disorder.

___ 10. Which sentence is **not** relevant support for the argument that genetic testing should be limited?
  A. Sentence 1   C. Sentence 8
  B. Sentence 6   D. Sentence 10

CRITICAL READING: Test A (Fact and Opinion)

A. Five of the statements below are facts, and five are opinions. In addition, two statements include both fact and opinion. Identify facts with an **F**, opinions with an **O**, and each statement of fact *and* opinion with an **F+O**.

_____ 1. In 1939, there were fewer than two thousand private TV sets in the entire United States.

_____ 2. School-age children should watch television for no more than one hour a day.

_____ 3. Television is as addictive as any drug on the market today.

_____ 4. Despite the popularity of television, booksellers across the country have reported record sales in recent years.

_____ 5. The growing popularity of television and electronic books will eventually close all bookstores.

_____ 6. Games of chance should be made illegal everywhere except in casinos.

_____ 7. Poker is appealing because it is simple to learn; can be played by two to ten players; and, best of all, is played for serious money.

_____ 8. For over a century, a backstage game of poker has been going on during intermission at the Metropolitan Opera in New York City.

_____ 9. When abolitionist Abby Kelly requested permission to speak at the meeting of the Connecticut Anti-Slavery Society in 1840, the members voted to grant her permission.

_____ 10. The chairman of the Connecticut Anti-Slavery Society meeting immediately resigned his post with the declaration that he would not preside over a group that allowed women to speak.

_____ 11. To inspire pride and good citizenship in our nation's children, every student should travel to Washington, D.C., and visit the Smithsonian Museum at least once.

_____ 12. The Smithsonian, a national treasure, is a collection of museums that care for 140 million items, including such wonderful memorabilia as Dorothy's ruby slippers from *The Wizard of Oz*.

B. Following are two textbook passages. Identify each listed statement from the passage as either fact (**F**), the author's opinion (**O**), or fact *and* opinion (**F+O**). Only one statement combines fact and opinion.

   ¹Some workplaces have instituted a casual day, often Fridays, when the official or unofficial dress code is relaxed or abandoned. ²This is not necessarily a blessing. ³Even though the standards of attire are supposedly lowered, what you wear will still be scrutinized. ⁴Now, instead of business wear and casual, you may need attire that falls in

(Continues on next page)

between these two—something that is now being called "business casual." [5]Also, although the dress restrictions have been eased, this is often done only for those with no client contact. [6]This means that people must check the calendar (to see if it is a casual day) and their schedules (to see if they have outside appointments) before getting dressed in the morning. [7]Although this is a concern, casual dress also has some problems. [8]For many companies, a large problem is that workers have taken the casual concept too far. [9]Workers have come to work in sweatsuits, shorts, and spandex. [10]Another drawback to casual dress, some say, is that it also leads to casual attitudes. [11]One firm found its sales staff felt that casual day was a "no sales call" day; instead of getting one relaxed dress day, the firm got one less work day. [12]The policy was soon reversed.

_____ 13. [A relaxed or abandoned dress code] is not necessarily a blessing.

_____ 14. Workers have come to work in sweatsuits, shorts, and spandex.

_____ 15. Another drawback to casual dress, some say, is that it also leads to casual attitudes.

[1]Ernesto Miranda was hardly the kind of person to influence legal history, but he did, in his own savage way, because of legal efforts on his behalf. [2]A high-school dropout with a criminal record dating to his teen years, Miranda abducted a teenage girl at a Phoenix movie house candy counter in 1963 and drove her into the desert, where he raped her. [3]After being picked up and making a written confession in which he stated that he had been informed of his rights, Miranda was convicted and sentenced to forty to fifty-five years in prison. [4]Society would have been better off if he had stayed there. [5]But at the trial, Miranda's court-appointed lawyer argued that his client had not been told of his right to legal counsel.

[6]The American Civil Liberties Union took the case of *Miranda v. Arizona* all the way to the Supreme Court, where it was heard by the Warren Court in 1966. [7]On June 13, 1966, the Court announced a five-to-four ruling in favor of Miranda that said a criminal suspect must be told of his right to silence, that his remarks may be used against him, and that he had a right to counsel during questioning, even if he could not afford one.

[8]Many citizens hailed this announcement as a great milestone for civil liberties and the protection of the rights of both the innocent and the criminal. [9]Yet it was hard to be happy when a convicted rapist had gone free.

[10]Fortunately, justice was eventually served in the *Miranda* case. [11]Based on new evidence, Miranda was convicted on the same charges of kidnapping and rape, and imprisoned. [12]He was eventually paroled, and ten years after the Court inscribed his name in legal history, Ernesto Miranda died of a knife wound suffered during a bar fight.

_____ 16. Ernesto Miranda was hardly the kind of person to influence legal history, but he did, in his own savage way, because of legal efforts on his behalf.

_____ 17. A high-school dropout with a criminal record dating to his teen years, Miranda abducted a teenage girl at a Phoenix movie house candy counter in 1963 and drove her into the desert, where he raped her.

_____ 18. Society would have been better off if he had stayed there.

_____ 19. The American Civil Liberties Union took the case of *Miranda v. Arizona* all the way to the Supreme Court, where it was heard by the Warren Court in 1966.

_____ 20. He was eventually paroled, and ten years after the Court inscribed his name in legal history, Ernesto Miranda died of a knife wound suffered during a bar fight.

CRITICAL READING: Test B (Propaganda Techniques)

A. Each pair of items below illustrates a particular propaganda technique. On the line next to each pair, write the letter of the main technique being used.

_____ 1. • A group of adorable golden retriever puppies tumble over one another as an announcer says, "This happy moment is brought to you by Horizon Financial Management."

• A sleek sports car pulls up to a fancy restaurant. A beautiful woman in a short black dress emerges. As she closes the car door, the camera focuses on the gold watch on her wrist. The brand name of the watch flashes on the screen.

    A. Glittering generalities   C. Transfer
    B. Testimonial   D. Bandwagon

_____ 2. • The slogan for a boxed cake mix is "You can taste the love in every bite."

• A commercial for hair color ends with the words, "Love the life you're in."

    A. Testimonial   C. Transfer
    B. Glittering generalities   D. Name calling

_____ 3. • An ad for Dewy skin moisturizer says, "Dewy works hard for you all day. Other moisturizers are just plain lazy."

• A local restaurant advertises, "If you want freezer-burned microwaved meals, by all means eat at Jim's Diner. But if you want freshly prepared food, come to us."

    A. Name calling   C. Bandwagon
    B. Plain folks   D. Transfer

_____ 4. • A state senator makes an ad in favor of a health-care reform bill. He is shown in his living room with his elderly grandmother. "I'm supporting this bill," he says, "because it's good for people like Nana."

• A man in work clothes is shown chatting with other workers on an automobile assembly line. He says, "We auto workers are all in this together – whether you're a line worker like Stan here, or the president of the company like me."

    A. Transfer   C. Plain folks
    B. Glittering generalities   D. Testimonial

(Continues on next page)

_____ 5. • At a table full of kids, a little boy holds up a tall plastic container with a straw in it and exclaims, "Nine out of ten kids agree—Slimy Slurpees are the best thirst-quencher money can buy!"

• A TV ad shows a crowd of people rushing down a street. "Where is everybody going?" asks a woman on the sidewalk. People in the crowd shout back, "To get the great deals at Hanahan & Sons Furniture!"

A. Testimonial   C. Transfer
B. Name calling   D. Bandwagon

_____ 6. • An action movie star is shown hurrying to an appointment and jumping into a rental car. "When my superpowers aren't available, I count on Dependable Auto Rental to get me where I need to go."

• A woman is shown hugging her toddler son. She says, "On July 15 of last year, the Safe-T swimming pool alarm system saved my little boy's life."

A. Testimonial   C. Transfer
B. Name calling   D. Glittering generalities

B. Below are descriptions of four actual ads. On each line, write the letter of the main propaganda technique that applies to the ad.

A Bandwagon	D Plain folks
B Testimonial	E Name calling
C Transfer	F Glittering generalities

_____ 7. An ad for the Motorola Droid smartphone compares it with the Apple iPhone. It points out the failings of the Apple phone, calling it the "iDon't."

_____ 8. Over the song "Everyday People," Toyota shows shots of kids swimming, people on farms, a lobster fisherman, lumberjacks, etc., with the final line being "Toyota owners: everyday people."

_____ 9. A recent ad campaign for Coca-Cola uses the slogan, "Open Happiness."

_____ 10. Actress Lorraine Bracco, who formerly played a psychiatrist on HBO's _The Sopranos_, appears in advertising for the drug company Pfizer, Inc., in which she encourages people to seek treatment for depression.

CRITICAL READING: Test C (Errors in Reasoning)

A. Each pair of items below illustrates a particular error in reasoning. On the line next to each item, write the letter of the logical fallacy contained in both items. Choose from the three fallacies shown in the box below.

> A Circular reasoning (*a statement repeats itself rather than providing a real supporting reason to back up an argument*)
> B Personal attack (*ignores the issue under discussion and concentrates instead on the character of the opponent*)
> C Straw man (*an argument is made by claiming an opponent holds an extreme position and then opposing that extreme position*)

_____ 1. • The mayor is asking us not to water our lawns because of the drought. Pretty soon she'll be telling us what we can wear and how much TV we're allowed to watch.

   • The police chief is cracking down on officers who don't tell suspects their rights when they're arrested. Obviously, he cares more about the rights of criminals than he does about their victims.

_____ 2. • Vegetables are a healthy addition to any diet because they're so good for you.

   • I'll never forget my third-grade teacher, Mrs. Cope, because she was the most unforgettable teacher I ever had.

_____ 3. • Who cares if he's the most famous athlete in the world? He shouldn't be allowed to compete in any more tournaments. He's just confessed to having several extramarital affairs.

   • How can that man teach high school biology? His own daughter attends a special school for emotionally disturbed teens.

_____ 4. • Michael Jordan was a tremendous basketball player because of his amazing athletic abilities.

   • My cousin's husband has hit her on several occasions due to the fact that he's abusive.

_____ 5. • The church intends to open a soup kitchen on Archer Street, but do we really want a magnet for derelicts in our neighborhood?

   • My neighbors are planning a trip to China this summer. It must not matter to them that China has a miserable human rights record.

(Continues on next page)

B. In the space provided, write the letter of the fallacy contained in each pair of arguments. Choose from the three fallacies shown in the box below.

> **A** False cause (*the argument assumes that the order of events alone shows cause and effect*)
>
> **B** False comparison (*the argument assumes that two things being compared are more alike than they really are*)
>
> **C** Either-or (*the argument assumes that there are only two sides to a question*)

_____ 6. • The last time my cousins visited, I got a migraine headache that lasted for two days. I'm never inviting them again.

• Our neighbors' son is always in trouble with the law. It's no wonder; he listens to heavy metal music all the time.

_____ 7. • Both puppies and children are little—and sometimes naughty. So when my kids misbehave, I hit them gently with a rolled-up newspaper.

• My dad ate eggs fried in butter and bacon for breakfast every day, and he lived to be 93, so I can't see what all the fuss about cholesterol is about.

_____ 8. • Either you give me your notes from the lectures I skipped, or I'll know that you aren't really my friend.

• Are you working part-time while you go to college, or are you sponging off your parents?

_____ 9. • My girlfriend said my essay was extremely well written, so I'm sure my instructor will give it an A.

• Guns are dangerous, and crowbars are dangerous. But nobody tries to outlaw crowbars, so they shouldn't outlaw guns.

_____10. • Reading too much can make you crazy. I knew a very well-educated man who had serious mental problems.

• I wore my leather jacket and black Converse sneakers when I took my last math test, and I got an A. Of course, I'm going to wear the same outfit the next time there's a test!

CRITICAL READING: Test D

A. Read the following textbook passage. Then identify each listed excerpt from the passage as either a fact (**F**), an opinion (**O**), or a combination of fact *and* opinion (**F+O**).

[1]Every new nation needs a hero to survive. [2]George Washington's greatest contribution to the young United States was that he was a larger-than-life hero. [3]Indeed, only in recent times have Washington's life and accomplishments been looked at in a new light. . . .

[4]Traditionalists say that, as commander, Washington held together a ragged, ill-equipped army by sheer force of will, chose his commanders well, and became a master of the strategic retreat. [5]But traditionalists have believed too many popular myths. [6]The revisionist view holds that Washington was an overly harsh leader who maintained brutal discipline in the ranks, nearly lost the war several times, and was saved only by greater incompetence on the part of the British.

[7]After serving as president for eight years, he returned to the gentleman's life at Mount Vernon, where he caught a chill on a cold December day. [8]Left alone, he might have survived. [9]Instead his physicians bled him, standard medical procedure in the day, and the treatment probably doomed him.

_____ 1. George Washington's greatest contribution to the young United States was that he was a larger-than-life hero.

_____ 2. After serving as president for eight years, he returned to the gentleman's life at Mount Vernon, where he caught a chill on a cold December day.

_____ 3. Instead his physicians bled him, standard medical procedure in the day, and the treatment probably doomed him.

B. Below are three items. On each line, write the letter of the main propaganda technique that applies to the item

A	Bandwagon	D	Plain folks
B	Testimonial	E	Name calling
C	Transfer	F	Glittering generalities

_____ 4. A critic of the president's health-care reform ideas calls him a "socialist."

_____ 5. An ad for a gambling casino invites visitors to "experience the rainbow."

_____ 6. In a television ad, a worried-looking older couple sit sifting through a pile of bills. "Medical insurance is so confusing these days!" says the woman. "Maybe we should call Medical Coverage Consultants for a free consultation."

(Continues on next page)

C. In the space provided, write the letter of the fallacy contained in each pair of arguments. Choose from the three fallacies shown in the box below.

> **A** Circular reasoning (*a statement repeats itself rather than providing a real supporting reason to back up an argument*)
> **B** Personal attack (*ignores the issue under discussion and concentrates instead on the character of the opponent*)
> **C** Straw man (*an argument is made by claiming an opponent holds an extreme position and then opposing that extreme position*)

_____ 7. • The Grand Canyon is a popular tourist destination because so many people go there.

• Green Bay Packers Coach Vince Lombardi was famous for his ability to inspire his players because of the way he motivated them to succeed.

_____ 8. • I'd never go to Dr. Fuentes for medical care. When she had her first baby, she was only 16 and unmarried.

• Our member of Congress is clearly not qualified for office. He admits he's taken anti-depressant medication for years.

D. In the space provided, write the letter of the fallacy contained in each pair of arguments. Choose from the three fallacies shown in the box below.

> **A** False cause (*the argument assumes that the order of events alone shows cause and effect*)
> **B** False comparison (*the argument assumes that two things being compared are more alike than they really are*)
> **C** Either-or (*the argument assumes that there are only two sides to a question*)

_____ 9. • Are you against the war in Afghanistan, or do you want the terrorists to win?

• Unless you limit your child's TV viewing to an hour per day, you're not really serious about helping him succeed in school.

_____ 10. • I filled up my car at the Luxo station on Route 363, and the next day my tank sprang a leak. I'll certainly never buy gas there again.

• The McNeills' adopted son, Rudy, just got arrested for possessing marijuana. That's what happens when you adopt a child from a foreign country.

COMBINED SKILLS: Test A

After reading the passage, write the letter of the best answer to each question.

[1]The eyes themselves can send several kinds of messages. [2]Meeting someone's glance with your eyes is usually a sign of involvement, whereas looking away often signals a desire to avoid contact. [3]This is why solicitors on the street—panhandlers, salespeople, petitioners—try to catch our eye. [4]Once they've managed to establish contact with a glance, it becomes harder for the approached person to draw away. [5]Most of us remember trying to avoid a question we didn't understand by glancing away from the teacher. [6]At times like these we usually became very interested in our textbooks, fingernails, the clock—anything but the teacher's stare. [7]Of course, the teacher always seemed to know the meaning of this nonverbal behavior, and ended up calling on those of us who signaled our uncertainty.

[8]Another kind of message the eyes communicate is a positive or negative attitude. [9]When someone glances toward us with the proper facial expression, we get a clear message that the looker is interested in us—hence the expression "making eyes." [10]At the same time, when our long glances toward someone else are avoided by that person, we can be pretty sure that the other person isn't as interested in us as we are in him or her. [11](Of course, there are all sorts of courtship games in which the receiver of a glance pretends not to notice any message by glancing away, yet signals interest with some other part of the body.)

[12]The eyes communicate both dominance and submission. [13]We've all played the game of trying to stare somebody down, and in real life there are also times when downcast eyes are a sign of giving in. [14]In some religious orders, for example, subordinate members are expected to keep their eyes downcast when addressing a superior.

____ 1. The word *solicitors* in sentence 3 means
   A. panhandlers.
   B. people who pass by.
   C. people who wish to ask for something.
   D. people who wish to help us.

____ 2. The word *subordinate* in sentence 14 means
   A. below another in rank or power.
   B. more powerful than another.
   C. disrespectful.
   D. playful.

____ 3. According to the author, avoiding the eyes of someone who is giving us long glances
   A. is a sure sign of interest.
   B. is always an indication of lack of interest.
   C. indicates respect for someone with greater rank or power.
   D. usually, but not always, indicates a lack of interest.

(Continues on next page)

_____ 4. The relationship of sentence 8 to the sentences that precede it is one of
A. time.   C. illustration.
B. comparison.   D. addition.

_____ 5. The relationship of sentence 14 to sentence 13 is one of
A. addition.   C. illustration.
B. contrast.   D. comparison.

_____ 6. The main pattern of organization of this passage is
A. series of steps.
B. list of items.
C. comparison and/or contrast.
D. definition and example.

_____ 7. From this passage, you could infer that
A. people should communicate verbally more often.
B. eye messages can reflect our desires and relationships.
C. we should try to avoid communicating with our eyes.
D. eye messages are more likely to be negative than positive.

_____ 8. Which is the most appropriate title for this selection?
A. The Human Eye
B. The Role of Eyes in Courtship
C. The Eyes As Messengers
D. Using the Eyes to Establish Dominance

_____ 9. The topic sentence of the second paragraph is sentence
A. 8.   C. 10.
B. 9.   D. 11.

_____ 10. Which of the following best outlines the passage?
A. Types of messages sent by the eyes
    1. An interest or lack of interest in involvement
    2. A positive or negative attitude
    3. Dominance and submission

B. 1. Meeting someone's glance
      a. A sign of involvement
      b. Lack of involvement
   2. Positive attitude
      a. Making eyes
      b. Lack of interest—avoidance of glance
      c. Dominance—"staring somebody down"
      d. Submission—giving in

C. Nonverbal behavior
    1. Meeting someone's glance
    2. Avoiding someone's glance
    3. Staring others down
    4. Giving in

COMBINED SKILLS: Test B

After reading the passage, write the letter of the best answer to each question.

[1]When the *Mayflower* left Plymouth, England, in September 1620 on its historic journey to the New World, three of its 102 passengers were pregnant. [2]The fates of the three pregnant women and their children illustrate the fears that early American women facing childbirth must have held for themselves as well as for their children's survival. [3]One of the passengers, Elizabeth Hopkins, gave birth at sea to a baby boy she named Oceanus. [4]Oceanus Hopkins died during the Pilgrims' first winter in Plymouth. [5]Two weeks after Oceanus's birth, *Mayflower* passenger Susanna White bore her son, Peregrine, who lived into his eighties. [6]The spring after the *Mayflower* arrived in Plymouth, passenger Mary Norris Allerton died giving birth to a stillborn baby.

[7]During the seventeenth and eighteenth centuries, nearly one and one-half percent of all births resulted in the death of the mother from exhaustion, infection, dehydration, or hemorrhage. [8]Since the typical mother gave birth to between five and eight children in her lifetime, her chances of dying in childbirth ran as high as one in eight. [9]Even when the mother survived childbirth, she had reason to be anxious about the fate of her child. [10]In even the healthiest seventeenth-century communities, one in ten children died before the age of 5. [11]Less healthy settlements saw three out of ten children dying in their early years.

____ 1. According to the author, the experience of the three pregnant *Mayflower* passengers and their babies
    A. was very unusual for that time period.
    B. demonstrated how safe ocean travel was in that era.
    C. was typical for that time period.
    D. is similar to the experience of today's women and infants.

____ 2. During the seventeenth century, childbirth in America was
    A. rare.
    B. dangerous.
    C. avoided.
    D. easy.

____ 3. According to the passage, early childhood in colonial America was a time of great
    A. health risk.
    B. hope.
    C. learning.
    D. exhaustion.

(Continues on next page)

____ 4. The first paragraph
  A. discusses a series of causes.
  B. lists the fates of three early American pregnant women and their children.
  C. discusses the similarities between three pregnant travelers and their children.
  D. narrates the events of the *Mayflower*'s journey.

____ 5. This passage is made up mainly of
  A. facts.
  B. opinions.

____ 6. From this passage, you could infer that
  A. all settlements were equally unhealthy.
  B. early American families tended to be smaller than they are now.
  C. antibiotics to control infection were not available in seventeenth-century America.
  D. all of the above.

____ 7. From the passage, you can conclude that in seventeenth-century America
  A. it was not unusual for men to become widowers.
  B. mothers were likely to have at least one child die by the age of five.
  C. women experienced frequent pregnancies.
  D. all of the above.

____ 8. The author's primary purpose in the passage is to
  A. question.
  B. praise.
  C. inform.
  D. entertain.

____ 9. The author's attitude toward the facts is
  A. fearful.
  B. shocked.
  C. objective.
  D. sorrowful.

____10. Which sentence best expresses the central point of the passage?
  A. Traveling on the *Mayflower* was dangerous for pregnant women and their babies.
  B. There were great health dangers involved with childbirth and childhood in early America.
  C. Women's health suffered greatly in colonial America.
  D. In the early American colonies, infant mortality was great.

COMBINED SKILLS: Test C

After reading the passage, write the letter of the best answer to each question.

[1]Modern crowds that flood museums to view fabled treasures of Egyptian art are still captivated by the spell of one of the oldest and most alluring civilizations in history. [2]Almost as old as the civilization founded in Mesopotamia during the fourth millennium B.C.E., Egyptian civilization provides a fascinating contrast to that of Mesopotamia because it was characterized by stability and serenity as opposed to the turmoil and tension of Mesopotamia. [3]Not only were the Egyptians peaceful for long periods of their ancient history, but surviving Egyptian statuary and painted human figures often seem to smile and bask in the sun as if they were on summer vacation.

[4]Environmental factors best explain the striking differences. [5]Since the Mesopotamian climate was harsh, and since the Tigris and Euphrates flooded irregularly, the Mesopotamians could not view nature as dependably life-enhancing. [6]Furthermore, since Mesopotamia, located on an open plain, was not geographically protected from foreign incursions, its inhabitants were necessarily on continual military alert. [7]Egyptian civilization, on the other hand, was centered on the dependably life-enhancing Nile. [8]Not only did the richly fertile soil of the Nile valley provide great agricultural wealth, but the Nile flooded regularly year after year during the summer months and always receded in time for a bountiful growing season, offering Egyptians the feeling that nature was predictable and benign. [9]In addition, since the Nile valley was surrounded by deserts and the Red Sea, Egypt was comparatively free from threats of foreign invasion.

____ 1. The word *enhancing* in sentences 5 and 7 means
   A. harming.
   B. improving.
   C. creating.
   D. questioning.

____ 2. The word *incursions* in sentence 6 means
   A. invasions.
   B. languages.
   C. supporters.
   D. delays.

____ 3. According to the passage, the Nile was
   A. more beautiful than the Tigris and Euphrates rivers.
   B. larger than the Tigris and Euphrates.
   C. more predictable than the Tigris and Euphrates.
   D. deeper than the Tigris and Euphrates.

(Continues on next page)

_____ 4. Sentence 5 expresses a relationship of
   A. addition.
   B. time.
   C. contrast.
   D. cause-effect.

_____ 5. The main pattern of organization of the passage is
   A. list of items.
   B. time order.
   C. comparison.
   D. contrast.

_____ 6. Sentence 1 is
   A. all fact.
   B. all opinion.
   C. a mixture of fact and opinion.

_____ 7. The passage suggests that the environment can affect
   A. war and peace.
   B. art.
   C. diet.
   D. all of the above.

_____ 8. We can conclude that civilizations grew up in river valleys because
   A. the valleys kept out foreign invaders.
   B. rivers provided water, which was essential for good crops.
   C. clothing could easily be washed in the nearby river.
   D. people could better defend themselves over water.

_____ 9. In sentence 1, the author's tone can be described as
   A. enthusiastic and admiring.
   B. serious and solemn.
   C. tolerant and hopeful.
   D. warm and affectionate.

_____ 10. Which sentence best expresses the central point of the passage?
   A. Museums are a doorway to fascinating ancient civilizations.
   B. Ancient civilizations tended to settle and flourish in fertile river valleys.
   C. While the Tigris and Euphrates flooded irregularly, the Nile River flooded regularly during the summer months.
   D. The Mesopotamians and Egyptians built two very different civilizations in large part because of the differences in their environments.

COMBINED SKILLS: Test D

After reading the passage, write the letter of the best answer to each question.

[1]Cells, like any factory, need energy to operate. [2]Two different kinds of cellular power plants have evolved: some cells absorb energy directly from the sun, while others gather energy by eating other organisms that have stored it. [3]Plants acquire energy directly from sunlight through the process of photosynthesis. [4]In this process, molecules of chlorophyll or related pigments absorb photons from the sun. [5]The photons' energy is converted into chemical energy that the plant can use to grow and reproduce. [6]In the course of this rather complicated chemical process, carbon dioxide and water from the cell's surroundings are converted into glucose plus oxygen. [7]The net effect of photosynthesis, then, is to remove carbon dioxide from the air, produce energy for the cell, and give off oxygen as a waste product. [8]Animals, unlike plants, cannot convert the sun's energy directly to food, and therefore must get theirs by eating plants or by eating animals that eat plants. [9]The food you eat contains energy in the form of the bonds that hold its molecules together. [10]After the food has been broken down, it is taken into the cells, where its energy is released by a process called respiration. [11]This process allows molecules like glucose to combine with oxygen, thereby releasing the energy tied up in the molecular bonds. [12]Its waste product is carbon dioxide, which you breathe out.

____ 1. The word *net* in sentence 7 means
    A. final.
    B. negative.
    C. unlikely.
    D. sensible.

____ 2. The energy in the food you eat
    A. is contained in the bonds that hold its molecules together.
    B. is absorbed into your body by photons.
    C. is released by your body in a process called photosynthesis.
    D. results in a waste product of oxygen, which you breathe out.

____ 3. TRUE OR FALSE? While plants give off carbon dioxide as a waste product of photosynthesis, animals give off carbon dioxide as a waste product of respiration.

____ 4. From sentence 4, we can deduce that the sun gives off
    A. chlorophyll.
    B. pigments.
    C. photons.
    D. all of the above.

(Continues on next page)

_____ 5. From sentences 10–12, we can deduce that respiration requires
  A. oxygen.
  B. photosynthesis.
  C. carbon dioxide.
  D. chlorophyll.

_____ 6. It can be inferred that glucose is
  A. important in the energy processes of both plants and animals.
  B. produced during photosynthesis.
  C. sometimes combined with oxygen during respiration.
  D. all of the above.

_____ 7. From the paragraph, we can infer that houseplants benefit humans by
  A. giving off oxygen.
  B. taking oxygen from the air.
  C. adding carbon dioxide to the air.
  D. adding both oxygen and carbon dioxide to the air.

_____ 8. The author's primary purpose is to
  A. entertain.
  B. persuade.
  C. inform.
  D. question.

_____ 9. The topic sentence of the passage is
  A. sentence 1.
  B. sentence 2.
  C. sentence 7.
  D. sentence 8.

_____ 10. Which outline best organizes the material in the passage?
  A. Kinds of cellular "power plants"
    1. Plant cells
    2. Animal cells

  B. Different kinds of cellular power plants
    1. Animals
    2. Plants
    3. Photosynthesis
    4. Respiration
    5. Glucose combined with oxygen

  C. Cells, like any factory, need energy to operate.
    1. Photons' energy is converted into chemical energy.
    2. Carbon dioxide is removed from the air.
    3. Animal cells release energy through respiration.

ANSWERS TO THE TESTS IN THE TEST BANK

VOCABULARY IN CONTEXT: Test A

1. Examples: *Duane is very shy while his brother is outgoing; Duane enjoys reading while his brother prefers playing sports;* A
2. Examples: *outbursts, quarrels;* D
3. skilled
4. careful and precise
5. disapproves
6. Antonym: *painstaking, thorough;* A
7. Antonym: *harmful;* D
8. D
9. B
10. D

VOCABULARY IN CONTEXT: Test B

1. Examples: *painted colorful circus pictures, pasted seashells;* C
2. Examples: *driving a taxi, writing books;* C
3. Examples: *spending hours on improving handwriting, memorizing the date each of the fifty states entered the union;* B
4. hostile
5. risky
6. Antonym: *praising;* B
7. Antonym: *prepared;* D
8. C
9. C
10. A

VOCABULARY IN CONTEXT: Test C

1. C		6.	A
2. C		7.	C
3. B		8.	A
4. A		9.	C
5. D		10.	D

VOCABULARY IN CONTEXT: Test D

1. D		6.	A
2. B		7.	B
3. C		8.	D
4. C		9.	D
5. D		10.	A

MAIN IDEAS: Test A

1. 1		4.	2
2. 5		5.	1
3. 6			

MAIN IDEAS: Test B

1. 2		4.	8
2. 3		5.	2
3. 7			

MAIN IDEAS: Test C

A.	1. 1		4.	10
	2. 7	B.	5.	2
	3. 2			

MAIN IDEAS: Test D

A.	1. 1		4.	3
	2. 3	B.	5.	16
	3. 1			

SUPPORTING DETAILS: Test A

A. (1–6.) *(Wording of answers may vary.)*
   Main idea: There are a few major reasons for family violence.
   1. Stress is highest among certain groups.
      a. Urban poor
   2. a. Violence on TV
      c. Death penalty
   3. Tendency for marital violence to be transmitted from one generation to the next

B. 7. B
   8. A
   9. B
   10. B

SUPPORTING DETAILS: Test B

A. (1–5.) *(Wording of answers may vary.)*
   Main idea: Suburbs can be divided into four distinct categories.

   Higher-income suburbs

   Affluent settled communities   Low-income growing communities   Low-income stagnant communities

B. 6. C
   7. A
   8. B
   9. C
   10. C

SUPPORTING DETAILS: Test C

A. 1. C
   2. A
   3. C
  4–5. (Wording of answers and example may vary.)
     Dominance hierarchy is a social arrangement in which animals establish a rank, eventually reducing aggression.
     Ex.—Chickens establishing a "pecking order"

B. (6–10.) (Wording of answers may vary.)
  Main idea: Relationships develop through five levels.
   1. Initiating
   3. Intensifying
   4. Integrating: Personalities begin to merge; people expect to see them together; each is able to predict other's behavior.
   5. Bonding: Participants make a formal commitment.

IMPLIED MAIN IDEAS: Test A

1. B   3. D
2. C   4. D

IMPLIED MAIN IDEAS: Test C

A. 1. A
   2. C
B. 3. Seaweed has a number of surprising uses. (Wording of answer may vary.)
   4. Writers describe the writing process in different ways. (Wording of answer may vary.)

RELATIONSHIPS I: Test A

A. 1. E Until   B. 6. For one thing
   2. B First of all   7. Another
   3. C other   8. also
   4. D third   9. Eventually
   5. A also   10. A

(Note: Wording of main ideas in Tests B–D may vary.)

RELATIONSHIPS I: Test C

1. B   7–10. *Main idea:* Social movements
2. B   can be classified into four types.
3. during *or*   1b. Violent, illegal
   after   2c. Civil rights movement *or*
4. B   women's movement *or*
5. A   ecology movement
6. A   4. Expressive movements

SUPPORTING DETAILS: Test D

A. 1. C   3. D
   2. B   4. B

B. (5–10.) (Wording of answers may vary.)
  Main idea: Kohlberg has described three levels of moral reasoning.

Preconventional morality	Autonomous moral principles
	Fully internal; recognize conflicts between moral standards; make own judgments on basis of right, fairness, justice
Typical ages: 4–10	Typical ages: after 10

IMPLIED MAIN IDEAS: Test B

1. A   3. A
2. C   4. B

IMPLIED MAIN IDEAS: Test D

A. 1. D
   2. B
B. 3. Envy and jealousy are two different emotions. *(Note: Wording of answer may vary.)*
C. 4. B

RELATIONSHIPS I: Test B

A. 1. One   7–10. *Main idea: Carl Rogers*
   2. Another   *suggests three condi-*
   3. Finally   *tions for* promoting
   4. A   personal growth.
   5. C   Genuineness: Acceptance
B. 6. A   Being open
                with feelings

RELATIONSHIPS I: Test D

1. B   8–10. *Main idea:* Various chemicals
2. B   in the brain stimulate love.
3. A   1. Pheromones—Promote
4. one *or* Another   sexual attraction in the
5. B   opposite sex
6. A   3. Endorphins
7. One *or* In
   addition *or* another *or* third

RELATIONSHIPS II: Test A

A. 1. C Even though
   2. D For instance   B.
   3. A As a result
   4. F Similarly
   5. B because of

   6. E However
   7. C
   8. A
   9. D
  10. B

RELATIONSHIPS II: Test B

A. 1. A
   2. example
B. 3. B
   4. Because [of] or led to
C. 5. C

   6. In contrast
D. 7. B
   8. cause or lead to
E. 9. C
  10. in like manner or similarly or but

RELATIONSHIPS II: Test C

(Wording of answers 2–5 and 7–10 may vary.)

A. 1. B

2–5. *Main idea:* There are two main reasons that keep women from reaching the executive suite.
1. Most women tend not to be in the "pipeline" positions that lead to the top because of the male corporate culture.
  b. Men stereotype women as better at providing "support."
2. Most women lack mentors to teach them how to reach the top.

B. 6. A

7–10. *Main idea:* Mutualism is a relationship in which two organisms live together or cooperate for mutual benefit.

Are able to digest food	Predators are attacked; competing plants are destroyed	Are housed in thorns; get food

RELATIONSHIPS II: Test D

A. 1. C

2–5. *(Wording of answers may vary.)*
Main idea: Various reasons explain the rapid population growth in Europe from 1800–1870.
1. b. Curbing of cholera through sanitary reforms
2. Less undernourishment
3. Earlier marriages

B. 6. B

7–10. *(Wording of answers may vary.)*
Main idea: There are differences *between presidents and prime ministers.*

Selected from among people already in Parliament

Chooses cabinet members from outside Congress

No guaranteed majority

INFERENCES: Test A

A. 1. C
   2. C
   3. B

   4. C
B. 1, 2, 5, 6, 8, 10

INFERENCES: Test B

A. 1. C
   2. B
   3. B

   4. C
   5. B
B. 2, 4, 6, 8, 10

INFERENCES: Test C

A. 3, 4, 6, 8, 10
B. 3, 4, 5, 8, 10

INFERENCES: Test D

A. 2, 4, 5, 7, 8, 9
B. 7. B
   8. C

   9. A
  10. B

PURPOSE AND TONE: Test A

A. 1. I
   2. E
   3. P
   4. I
   5. P

   6. E
B. 7. E
   8. C
   9. F
  10. A

PURPOSE AND TONE: Test B

A. 1. B
   2. I
   3. H
   4. C
   5. A

   6. J
   7. D
   8. F
B. 9. I
  10. P

PURPOSE AND TONE: Test C

A. 1. B
   2. A
B. 3. A
   4. D

C. 5. C
   6. C
D. 7. B
   8. A

PURPOSE AND TONE: Test D

A. 1. C
   2. D
B. 3. B
   4. C

C. 5. C
   6. B
D. 7. B
   8. A

ARGUMENT: Test A

A.
1. C
2. C
3. A

4. D
B. 5–7. B, D, F
8–10. A, C, F

ARGUMENT: Test B

A.
1. C
2. D
3. C

B. 4. B
5. C

ARGUMENT: Test C

A. 1–3. A, C, E
4–6. A, D, F
B. 7. B

C. 8. B
9. C
10. C

ARGUMENT: Test D

A. 1–3. B, D, F
4–6. A, C, F
B. 7. C

C. 8. C
9. A
10. D

CRITICAL READING: Test A

A.
1. F
2. O
3. O
4. F
5. O
6. O
7. F+O
8. F
9. F
10. F

11. O
12. F+O
B. 13. O
14. F
15. F
16. F+O
17. F
18. O
19. F
20. F

CRITICAL READING: Test B

A.
1. C
2. B
3. A
4. C
5. D

6. A
B. 7. E
8. D
9. F
10. B

CRITICAL READING: Test C

A.
1. C
2. A
3. B
4. A
5. C

B. 6. A
7. B
8. C
9. B
10. A

CRITICAL READING: Test D

A.
1. O
2. F
3. F+O
B. 4. E
5. F

6. D
C. 7. A
8. B
9. C
10. A

COMBINED SKILLS: Test A

1. C
2. A
3. D
4. D
5. C

6. B
7. B
8. C
9. A
10. A

COMBINED SKILLS: Test B

1. C
2. B
3. A
4. B
5. A

6. C
7. D
8. C
9. C
10. B

COMBINED SKILLS: Test C

1. B
2. A
3. C
4. D
5. D

6. C
7. D
8. B
9. A
10. D

COMBINED SKILLS: Test D

1. A
2. A
3. F
4. C
5. A

6. D
7. A
8. C
9. B
10. A